BLOODY TIMES

THE FUNERAL OF ABRAHAM LINCOLN AND THE MANHUNT FOR JEFFERSON DAVIS

JAMES L. SWANSON

BLOODY TIMES

THE FUNERAL OF ABRAHAM LINCOLN AND THE MANHUNT FOR JEFFERSON DAVIS

Collins

An Imprint of HarperCollinsPublishers

Collins is an imprint of HarperCollins Publishers.

Bloody Times: The Funeral of Abraham Lincoln and the Manhunt for Jefferson Davis
Copyright © 2011 by James L. Swanson
All rights reserved. Printed in the United States of America.

Library of Congress Cataloging-in-Publication Data is available.
ISBN 978-0-06-156089-7

Typography by Tom Forget
10 11 12 13 14   LP/RRDH   10 9 8 7 6 5 4 3 2 1
❖
First Edition

BLOODY TIMES

THE FUNERAL OF ABRAHAM LINCOLN AND THE MANHUNT FOR JEFFERSON DAVIS

PROLOGUE

In the spring of 1865, the country was divided in two: the Union in the North, led by Abraham Lincoln, fighting to keep the Southern states from seceding from the United States. The South, led by its president, Jefferson Davis, believed it had the absolute right to quit the Union in order to preserve its way of life, including the right to own slaves. The bloody Civil War had lasted four years and cost 620,000 lives. In April 1865, the war was about to end.

INTRODUCTION

In April of 1865, as the Civil War drew to a close, two men set out on very different journeys. One, Jefferson Davis, president of the **Confederate** States of America, was on the run, desperate to save his family, his country, and his cause. The other, Abraham Lincoln, murdered on April 14, was bound for a different destination: home, the grave, and everlasting glory.

Today everybody knows the name of Abraham Lincoln. But before 1858, when Lincoln ran for the **United States Senate** (and lost the election), very few people had heard of him. Most people of those days would have recognized the name of Jefferson Davis. Many would have predicted Davis, not Lincoln, would become president of the United States someday.

Born in 1808, Jefferson Davis went to private schools and studied at a university, then moved on to the United States Military Academy at West Point. A fine horseback rider, he looked elegant in the saddle. He served as an officer in the United States army on the western frontier, and then became a planter, or a farmer, in Mississippi and was later elected a **United States Congress**man and later a senator. As a colonel in the Mexican-American War, he was wounded in battle and came home a hero.

Davis knew many of the powerful leaders of his time, including presidents Zachary Taylor and Franklin Pierce. He was a polished speech maker with a beautiful speaking voice. Put simply, he was well-known, respected, and admired in both the North and the South of the country.

What Davis had accomplished was even more remarkable because he was often ill. He was slowly going blind in one eye, and he periodically suffered from **malaria**, which gave him fevers, as well as a painful condition called **neuralgia**. He and his young wife, Sarah Knox Taylor, contracted malaria shortly after they were married. She succumbed to the disease. More than once he almost died. But his strength and his will to live kept him going.

Abraham Lincoln's life started out much different from Jefferson Davis's. Born in 1809, he had no wealthy relatives to help give him a start in life. His father was a farmer who could not read or write and who gave Abe an ax at the age of nine and sent him to split logs into rails for fences. His mother died while Lincoln was still a young boy. When his father remarried, Abe's stepmother, Sarah, took a special interest in Abe.

By the time Abe Lincoln grew up, he'd had less than a year of school. But he'd managed to learn to read and write, and he wanted a better life for himself than that of a poor farmer. He tried many different kinds of jobs: piloting a riverboat, surveying (taking careful measurement of land to set up boundaries), keeping a store, and working as a postmaster.

He read books to teach himself law so that he could practice as an attorney. Finally in 1846 he was elected to the U.S. Congress. He served an unremarkable term, and at the end of two years, he left Washington and returned to Illinois and his law office. He was hardworking, well-off, and respected by the people who knew him—but not nearly as well-known or as widely admired as Jefferson Davis.

It may seem that two men could not be more different than Abraham Lincoln and Jefferson Davis. But in fact, they had many things in common. Both Davis and Lincoln loved books and reading. Both had children who died young. One of Davis's sons, Samuel, died when he was still a baby, and another, Joseph, died after an accident while Davis was the president of the Confederacy. Lincoln, too, lost one son, Eddie, at a very young age and another, Willie, his favorite, while he was president of the United States.

Both men fell in love young, and both lost the women they loved to illness. When he was twenty-four years old, Davis fell for Sarah Knox Taylor. Called Knox, she was just eighteen and was the daughter of army general and future president Zachary Taylor. It took Davis two years to convince her family to allow her to marry him—but at last he did. Married in June of 1835, just three months later both he and Knox fell ill with malaria, and she died. Davis was devastated. His grief changed him—afterward he was quieter, sterner, a different man.

Eight years later, he found someone else to love. He married Varina Howell, the daughter of a wealthy family. For the rest of his life, Davis would depend on Varina's love, advice, and loyalty. They would eventually have six children; only two would outlive Jefferson Davis.

Lincoln was still a young man when he met and fell in love with Ann Rutledge. Everyone expected them to get married, but before that could happen, Ann became ill and died. Lincoln himself never talked or wrote about Ann after her death. But those who knew him at the time remembered how crushed and miserable he was to lose her. Some even worried that he might kill himself.

Abraham Lincoln recovered and eventually married Mary Todd. But their marriage was not as happy as that of Jefferson and Varina. Mary was a woman of shifting moods. Jealous, insulting, rude, selfish, careless with money, she was difficult to live with.

By far the greatest difference between Davis and Lincoln was their view on slavery. Davis, a slave owner, firmly believed that white people were superior to blacks, and that slavery was good for black people, who needed and benefited from having masters to rule over them. He also believed that the founding fathers of the United States, the men who had written the **Constitution** and the **Declaration of Independence**, a number of whom had owned slaves, had intended slavery to be part of America forever.

Lincoln thought slavery was simply wrong, and he believed that the founders hadn't intended it always to exist in the United States. Lincoln was willing to let slavery remain legal in the states where it was already permitted. But he thought that slavery should not be allowed to spread into the new states entering the Union in the American south and southwest. Every new state to join the country, Lincoln firmly believed, should prohibit slavery.

Lincoln explained his views in several famous debates during his campaign for Senate in 1858. The campaign debates between Lincoln and Stephen Douglas brought Lincoln to national attention for the first time. Though he lost that Senate race, his new visibility enabled Lincoln to win the presidential nomination and election in 1860. To the surprise of many, it was Abraham Lincoln who became the president of the United States by winning less than 40 percent of the popular vote. More people voted for the other three candidates running for president than for Lincoln.

Oil portrait of Lincoln as he appeared on the eve of victory in 1865.

CHAPTER ONE

On the morning of Sunday, April 2, 1865, Richmond, Virginia, capital city of the Confederate States of America, did not look like a city at war. The White House of the Confederacy was surprisingly close to—one hundred miles from—the White House in Washington, D.C. But the armies of the North had never been able to capture Richmond. After four years of war, Richmond had not been invaded by Yankees. The people there had thus far been spared many of the horrors of fighting. This morning everything appeared beautiful and serene. The air smelled of spring, and fresh green growth promised a season of new life.

As he usually did on Sundays, President Jefferson Davis walked from his mansion to St. Paul's Episcopal Church. One of the worshippers, a young woman named Constance Cary, recalled the day: "On the Sunday morning of April 2, a perfect Sunday of the Southern spring, a large congregation assembled as usual at St. Paul's." As the service went on, a messenger entered the church. He brought Jefferson

Davis a telegram from Robert E. Lee.

The telegram was not addressed to Davis, but to his secretary of war, John C. Breckinridge. Breckinridge had sent it on to Davis. It told devastating news: The **Union** army was approaching the city gates, and the Army of Northern Virginia, with Lee in command, was powerless to stop them.

Headquarters, April 2, 1865

General J. C. Breckinridge:

> *I see no prospect of doing more than holding our position here till night. I am not certain that I can do that. . . . I advise that all preparation be made for leaving Richmond tonight. I will advise you later, according to circumstances.*
>
> *R. E. Lee*

On reading the telegram, Davis did not panic, but he turned pale and quietly rose to leave the church. The news quickly spread through Richmond. "As if by a flash of electricity, Richmond knew that on the morrow her streets would be crowded by her captors, her rulers fled . . . her high hopes crushed to earth," Constance Cary wrote later. "I saw many pale faces, some trembling lips, but in all that day I heard no expression of a weakling fear."

Many people did not believe that Richmond would be captured. General Lee would not allow it to happen, they told themselves. He would protect the city, just as the army had before. In the spring of 1865, Robert E. Lee was the greatest hero in the Confederacy, more popular than Jefferson Davis, who many people blamed for their country's present misfortunes. With Lee to defend them, many people of Richmond refused to believe that before the sun rose the next morning, life as they knew it would come to an end.

Jefferson Davis walked from St. Paul's to his office. He summoned the leaders of his government to meet with him there at once. Davis explained to his **cabinet** that the fall of Richmond would not mean the death of the Confederate States of America. He would not stay behind to surrender the capital. If Richmond was doomed to fall, then the president and the government would leave the city, travel south, and set up a new capital in Danville, Virginia, 140 miles to the southwest. The war would go on.

Jefferson Davis at the height of his power.

Davis told the cabinet to pack their most important records and send them to the railroad station. What they could not take, they must burn. The train would leave tonight, and he expected all of them to be on it. Secretary of War John C. Breckinridge would stay behind in Richmond to make sure the evacuation of the government went smoothly, and then follow the train to Danville. Davis ordered the train to take on other cargo, too: the Confederate **treasury**, consisting of half a million dollars in gold and silver coins.

After spending most of the afternoon working at his office, Davis walked home to pack his few remaining possessions. The house was eerily still. His wife, Varina, and their four children had already evacuated to Charlotte, North Carolina. His private secretary, Burton Harrison, had gone with them to make sure they reached safety.

Varina had begged to stay with her husband in Richmond until the end. Jefferson said no, that for their safety, she and the children must go. He understood that she wanted to help and comfort him, he told her, "but you can do this in but one way, and that is by going yourself and taking our children to a place of safety." What he said next was frightening: "If I live," he promised, "you can come to me when the struggle is ended."

On March 29, the day before Varina and the children left Richmond, Davis gave his wife a revolver and taught her how to use it. He also gave her all the money he had, saving just one five-dollar gold piece for himself. Varina and the children left the White House on Thursday, March 30. "Leaving the house as it was," Varina wrote later, "and taking only our clothing, I made ready with my young sister and my four little children, the eldest only nine years old, to go forth into the unknown." The children did not want to leave their father. "Our little Jeff begged to remain with him," Varina wrote, "and Maggie clung to him . . . for it was evident he thought he was looking his last upon us." The president took his family to the station and put them aboard a train.

While Jefferson Davis spent his last night in the Confederate White House, alone, without his family, he did not know that Abraham Lincoln had left his own White House several days ago and was now traveling in Virginia. Lincoln was visiting the Union army. The Union president did not want to go home until he had won the war. And he dreamed of seeing Richmond.

CHAPTER TWO

On March 23 at 1:00 P.M., Lincoln left Washington, bound south on the ship *River Queen*. His wife, Mary, came with him, along with their son Tad. A day later the vessel anchored off City Point, Virginia, headquarters of General Grant and the Armies of the United States.

Lincoln met with his commanders to discuss the war. General William Tecumseh Sherman asked Lincoln about his plans for Jefferson Davis. Many in the North wanted Davis hanged if he was captured. Did Lincoln think so, too? Lincoln answered Sherman by saying that all he wanted was for the Southern armies to be defeated. He wanted the Confederate soldiers sent back to their homes, their farms, and their shops. Lincoln didn't answer Sherman's question about Jefferson Davis directly. But he told a story.

There was a man, Lincoln said, who had sworn never to touch alcohol. He visited a friend who offered him a drink of lemonade. Then the friend suggested that the lemonade would taste better with a little brandy in it. The man replied that if some of the brandy were to get into the lemonade "unbeknown to him," that would be fine.

Sherman believed that Lincoln meant it would be the best thing for the country if Jefferson Davis were simply to leave and never return. As the Union president, Lincoln could hardly say in public that he wanted a man who had rebelled against his government to get away without punishment. But if Davis were to escape "unbeknown to him," as Lincoln seemed to be suggesting, that would be fine.

At City Point Lincoln received reports and sent messages. He haunted the army telegraph office for news of the battles raging in Virginia. He knew that soon Robert E. Lee must make a major decision: Would he sacrifice his army in a final, hopeless battle to defend Richmond, or would he abandon the Confederate capital and save his men to fight another day?

In the afternoon of April 2, Lee telegraphed another warning to Jefferson Davis in Richmond. "I think it absolutely necessary that we should abandon our position tonight," he wrote. Lee had made his choice. His army would retreat. Richmond would be captured.

Davis packed some clothes, retrieved important papers and letters from his private office, and waited at the mansion. Then a messenger brought him word: The officials of his government had assembled at the station. The train that would carry the president and the cabinet of the Confederacy was loaded and ready to depart.

Davis and a few friends left the White House, mounted their horses, and rode to the railroad station. Crowds did not line the streets to cheer their president or to shout best wishes for his journey. The citizens of Richmond were locking up their homes, hiding their valuables, or fleeing the city before the Yankees arrived. Throughout the day and into the night, countless people left however they could—on foot, on horseback, in carriages, in carts, or in wagons. Some rushed to the railroad station, hoping to catch the last train south. Few would escape.

But not all of Richmond's inhabitants dreaded the capital's fall. Among the blacks of Richmond, the mood was happy. At the African church, it was a day of jubilation. Worshippers poured into the streets, congratulated one another, and prayed for the coming of the Union army.

When Jefferson Davis got to the station, he hesitated. Perhaps the fortunes of war had turned in the Confederacy's favor that night. Perhaps Lee had defeated the enemy after all, as he had done so many times before. For an hour Davis held the loaded and waiting train in hopes of receiving good news from Lee. That telegram never came. The Army of Northern Virginia would not save Richmond from its fate.

Dejected, the president boarded the train. He did not have a private luxurious sleeping car built for the leader of a country. Davis took his seat in a common coach packed with the officials of his government. The train gathered steam and crept out of the station at slow speed, no more than ten miles per hour. It was a humble, sobering departure of the president of the Confederate States of America from his capital city.

As the train rolled out of Richmond, most of the passengers were somber. There was nothing left to say. "It was near midnight," Postmaster General John Reagan, on board the train, remembered, "when the President and his cabinet left the heroic city. As our train, frightfully overcrowded, rolled along toward Danville we were oppressed with sorrow for those we left behind us and fears for the safety of General Lee and his army."

The presidential train was not the last one to leave Richmond that night. A second one carried another cargo from the city—the treasure of the Confederacy, half a million dollars in gold and silver coins, plus deposits from the Richmond banks. Captain William Parker, an officer in the Confederate States Navy, was put in charge of the treasure and ordered to guard it during the trip to Danville. Men desperate to escape Richmond and who had failed to make it on to Davis's train climbed aboard their last hope, the treasure train. The wild mood at the station alarmed Parker, and he ordered his men—some were only boys—to guard the doors and not allow "another soul to enter."

Once Jefferson Davis was gone, and as the night wore on, Parker witnessed the breakdown of order: "The whiskey . . . was running in the gutters, and men were getting drunk upon it. . . . Large numbers of ruffians suddenly sprung into existence—I suppose thieves, deserters . . . who had been hiding." If the mob learned what cargo Parker and his men guarded, then the looters, driven mad by greed, would have attacked the train. Parker was prepared to order his men to fire on the crowd. Before that became necessary, the treasure train got up steam and followed Jefferson Davis into the night.

To add to the chaos caused by the mobs, soon there would be fire. And it would not be the Union troops who would burn the city. The Confederates accidentally set their own city afire when they burned supplies to keep them from Union hands. The flames spread out of control and reduced much of the capital to ruins.

The famous Currier and Ives print of Richmond burning, April 2, 1865.

Union troops outside Richmond would see the fire and hear the explosions. "About 2 o'clock on the morning of April 3d bright fires were seen in the direction of Richmond. Shortly after, while we were looking at these fires, we heard explosions," one witness reported.

On the way to Danville, the president's train stopped at Clover Station. It was three o'clock in the morning. There a young army lieutenant, eighteen years old, saw the train pull in. He spotted Davis through a window, waving to the people gathered at the station. Later he witnessed the treasure train pass, and others, too. "I saw a government on wheels," he said. From one car in the rear a man cried out, to no one in particular, "Richmond's burning. Gone. All gone."

As Jefferson Davis continued his journey to Danville, Richmond burned and Union troops approached. Around dawn a black man who had escaped the city reached Union lines and reported what Lincoln and U. S. Grant, the commanding general of the Armies of the United States, suspected. The Confederate government had abandoned the capital during the night and the road to the city was open. There would be no battle for Richmond. The Union army could march in and occupy the rebel capital without firing a shot.

The first Union troops entered Richmond shortly after sunrise on Monday, April 3. They marched through the streets, arrived downtown, and took control of the government buildings. They tried to put out the fires, which still burned in some sections of the city. Just a few hours since Davis had left it, the White House of the Confederacy was seized by the Union and made into their new headquarters.

CHAPTER THREE

The gloom that filled President Davis's train eased with the morning sun. Some of the officials of the Confederate government began to talk and tell jokes, trying to brighten the mood. Judah Benjamin, the secretary of state, talked about food and told stories. "[H]is hope and good humor [were] inexhaustible," one official recalled. With a playful air, he discussed the fine points of a sandwich, analyzed his daily diet given the food shortages that plagued the South, and as an example of doing much with little, showed off his coat and pants, both made from an old shawl, which had kept him warm through three winters. Colonel Frank Lubbock, a former governor of Texas, entertained his fellow travelers with wild western tales.

But back in Richmond, the people had endured a night of terror. The ruins and the smoke presented a terrible sight. A Confederate army officer wrote about what he saw at a depot, or warehouse, where food supplies were stored. "By daylight, on the 3d," he noted, "a mob of men, women, and children, to the number of several thousands, had gathered at the corner of 14th and Cary streets . . . for it must be remembered that in 1865 Richmond was a half-starved city, and the Confederate Government had that morning removed its guards and abandoned the removal of the provisions. . . . The depot doors were forced open and a demoniacal struggle for the countless barrels of hams, bacon, whisky, flour, sugar, coffee . . . raged about the buildings among the hungry mob. The gutters ran with whisky, and it was lapped up as it flowed down the streets, while all fought for a share of the plunder."

A Union officer wrote about what he saw as he entered the city in early morning, when it was still burning. "As we neared the city the fires seemed to increase in number and size, and at intervals loud explosions were heard. On entering the square we found Capitol Square covered with people who had fled there to escape the fire and were utterly worn out with **fatigue** and fright. Details were at once made to scour the city and press into service every able-bodied man, white or black, and make them assist in extinguishing the flames."

Constance Cary ventured outside to see her ruined and fallen city. Horrified, she discovered that Yankees had occupied the Confederate White House. "I looked over at the President's house, and saw the porch crowded with Union soldiers and politicians, the street in front filled with curious gaping negroes." The sight of ex-slaves roving freely about disgusted her. "It is no longer our Richmond," she complained, and added that the Confederate anthem still had the power to raise some people's spirits: "One of the girls tells me she finds great comfort in singing 'Dixie' with her head buried in a feather pillow."

All day on April 3, Washington, D.C., celebrated the fall of Richmond. The *Washington Star* newspaper captured the joyous mood: "As we write Washington city is in such a blaze of excitement and enthusiasm as we never before witnessed here. . . . The thunder of cannon; the ringing of bells; the eruption of flags from every window and housetop, the shouts of enthusiastic gatherings in the streets; all echo the glorious report. RICHMOND IS OURS!!!"

The Union capital celebrated without President Lincoln, who was

Broadside from the first week of April 1865.

still with the army. While Washington rejoiced, the secretary of war, Edwin Stanton, worried about Lincoln's safety. He believed that the president was traveling in enemy territory without sufficient protection. Stanton urged Lincoln to return to Washington. But Lincoln didn't take the warning. He telegraphed back:

> *Head Quarters Armies of the United States*
> *City-Point,*
> *April 3. 5 P.M. 1865*

> *Hon. Sec. of War*
> *Washington, D.C.*

> *Yours received. Thanks for your caution; but I have already been to Petersburg, stayed with Gen. Grant an hour & a half and returned here. It is certain now that Richmond is in our hands, and I think I will go there to-morrow. I will take care of myself.*
> *A. Lincoln*

President Davis did not arrive in Danville until 4:00 P.M. on the afternoon of April 3. It had taken eighteen hours to travel just 140 miles. The plodding journey from Richmond to Danville made clear an uncomfortable truth. If Jefferson Davis hoped to avoid capture, continue the war, and save the Confederacy, he would have to move a lot faster than this. Still, the trip had served its purpose. It had saved, for at least another day, the Confederate States of America.

On the afternoon and evening of Monday, April 3, the government on wheels unpacked and set up shop in Danville, Virginia. Jefferson Davis hoped to remain there as long as possible. In Danville he could send and receive communications so that he could issue orders and control the movements of his armies. It would be hard for his commanders to telegraph the president or send riders with the latest news if he stayed on the move and they had to chase him from town to town. In Danville he had the bare minimum he needed to continue the war.

The citizens of Danville had received word that their president was coming, and a large number of people waited at the station for his train. They cheered Jefferson Davis when he stepped down from his railroad car. The important people of the town opened their homes to the president and his government. But soon refugees fleeing from Richmond and elsewhere flooded into Danville. There was not enough room for everyone. Many slept in railroad cars and cooked their meals in the open.

But in Danville Davis and his government had little to do except wait for news. The future course of the war in Virginia depended upon Robert E. Lee and what was left of his army. Davis expected news from Lee on April 4, but none came. The president longed for action: He wanted to rally armies, send them to strategic places, and continue fighting. Instead, he had to sit still and wait for word from the Army of Northern Virginia.

"April 4 and the succeeding four days passed," noted Stephen R. Mallory, the secretary of the navy, "without bringing word from Lee or Breckinridge, or of the operations of the army; and the anxiety of the President and his followers was intense." Refugees from Richmond carried wild stories. Some said Lee had won "a glorious victory." Others said Lee was too busy fighting to send messengers. Jefferson Davis ignored the rumors.

★ ★ ★

On April 4, as Davis waited impatiently for news, Lincoln experienced one of the most thrilling days of his life. "Thank God that I have lived to see this!" he wrote. "It seems to me that I have been dreaming a horrid dream for four years, and now the nightmare is gone. I want to go to Richmond."

Admiral Porter, a Union navy admiral, agreed to take him there, "[i]f there is any of it left. There is black smoke over the city." On the *River Queen* they traveled up the river toward Richmond. When the water became too shallow for big boats, Porter transferred the president and Tad to his personal craft, the "admiral's barge." Despite the fancy name, it was no more than a big rowboat. But it allowed them to continue.

The city looked eerie. Lincoln and Porter peered at the rebel capital but saw no one. They saw smoke from the fires. The only sound was the creaking of the oars. "The street along the river-front was as deserted," Porter observed, "as if this had been a city of the dead." Although the Union army had controlled the city for several hours, "not a soldier was to be seen."

The oarsmen rowed for a wharf, and Lincoln stepped out of the boat. Admiral Porter described what happened next: "There was a small house on this landing, and behind it were some twelve negroes digging with spades. The leader of them was an old man sixty years of age. He raised himself to an upright position as we landed, and put his hands up to his eyes. Then he dropped his spade and sprang forward." The man knelt at Lincoln's feet, praising him, calling him the messiah come to free his children from slavery. "Glory, Hallelujah!" he cried, and kissed the president's feet. The others did the same.

Lincoln was embarrassed. He did not want to enter Richmond like a king. He spoke to the throng of former slaves. "Don't kneel to me.

That is not right. You must kneel to God only, and thank him for the liberty you will hereafter enjoy."

Before allowing Lincoln to leave them and proceed on foot into Richmond, the freed slaves burst into joyous song:

Oh, all ye people clap your hands,
And with triumphant voices sing;
No force the mighty power withstands
Of God, the universal King.

The hymn drew hundreds of blacks to the landing. They surrounded Lincoln, making it impossible for him to move. Admiral Porter recognized how foolish he had been to bring the president of the United States ashore without enough soldiers to protect him.

The crowd went wild. Some rushed forward, laid their hands upon the president, and collapsed in joy. Some, too awed to approach Father Abraham, kept their distance and, speechless, just stared at him. Others yelled for joy and performed somersaults. Lincoln spoke to them: "My poor friends, you are free—free as air. You can cast off the name of slave and trample upon it. . . . Liberty is your birthright. . . . But you must try to deserve this priceless boon. Let the world see that you merit it, and are able to maintain it by your good works. Don't let your joy carry you into excesses. Learn the laws and obey them. . . . There, now, let me pass on; I have but little time to spare. I want to see the capital."

Porter ordered six marines to march ahead of the president and six behind him, and the landing party walked toward downtown Richmond. The streets were dusty, and smoke from the fires still hung in the air. Lincoln could smell Richmond burning. By now thousands of people, blacks and whites, crowded the streets.

A beautiful girl, about seventeen years old, carrying a bouquet of roses, stepped into the street and advanced toward the president. Admiral Porter watched her struggle through the crowd. "She had a hard time in reaching him," he remembered. "I reached out and helped her within the circle of the sailors' bayonets, where, although nearly stifled with dust, she gracefully presented her bouquet to the President and made a neat little speech, while he held her hand. . . . There was a card on the bouquet with these simple words: 'From Eva to the Liberator of the slaves.'"

Porter spotted a sole soldier on horseback and called out to him: "Go to the general, and tell him to send a military escort here to guard the President and get him through this crowd!"

"Is that old Abe?" the trooper asked before galloping off.

Lincoln went on to the Confederate White House and entered Jefferson Davis's study. One of the men with him remembered watching Lincoln sit down and say, "'This must have been President Davis's chair.'" Lincoln crossed his legs and "looked far off with a serious, dreamy expression." Lincoln knew the Confederate president had been here, in this room, no more than thirty-six hours ago. This was the closest Abraham Lincoln had ever come to Jefferson Davis.

One observer remembered that Lincoln "lay back in the chair like a tired man whose nerves had carried him beyond his strength." Sitting in the quiet study of the Confederate president, perhaps Lincoln weighed the cost—more than 620,000 American lives—paid to get there. He did not speak. Then he requested a glass of water.

After Lincoln left the Confederate White House, he toured Richmond in a buggy. Blacks flocked to him and rejoiced, just as they had done at the river landing. But not all of Richmond welcomed him to the ruined capital. Most whites stayed in their homes behind locked doors and closed shutters, with some glaring at the unwelcome conqueror through their windows.

It was a miracle that no one poked a rifle or a pistol through an open window and opened fire on the despised Yankee president. Lincoln knew the risk. "I walked alone on the street, and anyone could have shot me from a second-story window," he said. His Richmond tour was one of Lincoln's triumphs. It was the most important day of his presidency. It was also one of the most dangerous days of his life. No American president before or since has ever placed himself at that much risk.

Before Lincoln left Richmond, the Union general left in charge of the city asked Lincoln to tell him how he should deal with the conquered rebels. Lincoln's answer became an American legend. He replied that he didn't want to give any orders, but, "If I were in your place I'd let 'em up easy, let 'em up easy."

During his time in Richmond, Lincoln did not order arrests of any rebel leaders who stayed in the city, did not order their property seized, and said nothing of vengeance or punishment. Nor did he order a manhunt for Davis and the officials who had left the city less than two days ago. It was a moment of remarkable greatness and generosity. It was Abraham Lincoln at his best.

CHAPTER FOUR

On the day Abraham Lincoln came to Richmond, Varina Davis reached Charlotte, North Carolina. Her journey had been miserable. "The baggage cars were all needing repairs and leaked badly. Our bedding was wet through by the constant rains that poured down." Varina, her children, and her small group of traveling companions settled into a rented house in Charlotte.

Jefferson Davis stayed in Danville for the next several days. He spent much of April 4, his first full day in Danville, sending and receiving messages. Bad news arrived from all over the Confederacy. "Selma [Alabama] has fallen—The Enemy threaten Montgomery [Alabama] and it is believed will march upon Columbus Georgia," one message read. Davis received more bad news from his nephew: "My Brigade was lost except about twenty men all captured; I went to Richmond to join you—arrived too late. . . . I deeply regret having missed you as I hoped in an humble way to have served you.

Remember me in love to aunt and the children."

Jefferson Davis's behavior once he reached Danville proved to the people of the South that he had not fled Richmond in a panicked bid to save his own life. If he had wanted to escape, even flee the country, Davis could have kept traveling south. Instead, he settled in Danville and prepared to continue the war. He wanted to show the people of the Confederacy that he had not abandoned them, that the cause was not lost, that he would never surrender, and that he would lead them to victory.

Davis realized that he must do more than set an example. He would, he decided, write a proclamation, a statement for the whole South to read. His most important task was to inspire Southerners to continue the war and to persuade them that, while the fall of Richmond was a terrible blow, it was not the death blow to their independence. "We have now entered upon a new phase of the struggle, the memory of which is to endure for all ages," he told them. "I announce to you, fellow countrymen, that it is my purpose to maintain your cause with my whole heart and soul; that I will never consent to abandon to the enemy one foot of the soil of any one of the States of the Confederacy. . . . Let us meet the foe with fresh defiance, with unconquered and unconquerable hearts."

April 4 was a day of two different messages from two different men. One man wanted to end the war and appealed to his people to "Let 'em up easy." The other man saw simply a "new phase of the struggle" and asked his people to never give up fighting.

Jefferson Davis also wrote a letter to Varina. "The people here have been very kind," he told her. "I do not wish to leave [Virginia], but cannot decide on my movements until those of the Army are better developed—I hope you are comfortable and trust soon to hear from you. Kiss my dear children—I weary of this sad recital and have nothing pleasant to tell."

Many Southerners agreed with Davis that the loss of Richmond did not mean the end of the war or the total defeat of the Confederacy. On April 6, Eliza Andrews, a twenty-four-year-old daughter of a lawyer and a plantation owner in Georgia, wrote in her diary. "I took a long walk through the village with Capt. Greenlaw after dinner, and was charmed with the lovely gardens and beautiful shade trees. On coming home, I heard of the fall of Richmond. Everybody feels very blue, but not disposed to give up as long as we have Lee."

And on April 6 Lee at last got in touch with Davis by telegraph. "I shall be tonight at Farmville," he told his president. "You can communicate by telegraph to Meherrin and by courier to Lynchburg." The Army of Northern Virginia was, President Davis believed, still prepared to fight, and that meant the war had not yet been lost.

But on April 7 Abraham Lincoln, still at City Point, had a different opinion. He sensed that Union victory was near. One of his generals told the president something that prompted him to telegraph U. S. Grant. It was time, Abraham Lincoln said, to close in for the kill and win the war.

Head Quarters Armies of the United States
City-Point,
April 7. 11 A.M. 1865

Lieut. Gen. Grant.
Gen. Sheridan says "If the thing is pressed I think that Lee will surrender." Let the *thing* *be pressed.*

A. Lincoln

Then Lincoln prepared to board the *River Queen* and return to Washington. Before he left, a United States army band played a farewell concert. At 11:00 P.M. the *River Queen* steamed away from City Point. Lincoln did not know it, but he was leaving a day too early. If only he could have read Robert E. Lee's mind, he would never have returned to Washington that night.

While Lincoln was on his way to Washington, Jefferson Davis had been in Danville for five days. He still refused to believe that Lee's Army of Northern Virginia was in danger of falling apart. But he was far from the battlefield and did not know what his most important general was thinking.

Lee believed that it might be impossible to continue fighting. He had hardly any men left and fit for battle—no more than several thousand. He was thinking of his surviving soldiers. The South would need them once the war was over. If the Confederacy was doomed to lose, could it be right to sacrifice any more lives?

On April 8 Lee sent a messenger to Danville with word for the president: He had little choice but to give up the fight. Then Lee composed a letter to Union general Ulysses S. Grant. The two generals would meet tomorrow.

Grant and Lee met on April 9 around 1:00 P.M. Neither Abraham Lincoln nor Jefferson Davis was there. In fact, neither president knew that the meeting was happening. While Lincoln sailed back to Washington and Davis waited in Danville for news, Ulysses S. Grant and Robert E. Lee met at the McLean house at Appomattox Court House, Virginia.

Grant treated Lee with courtesy, and he offered to accept the surrender of the Army of Northern Virginia on generous terms. Once the defeated men laid down their arms and agreed to fight no more, they would be free. They could wear their Confederate uniforms, take their horses, and just go home. They would not be made prisoners of war or be punished as traitors. And before men of the Army of Northern Virginia left the field for the final time, the Union soldiers paid honors to them. It was as Lincoln would have wished.

Abraham Lincoln arrived in Washington, D.C., at 6:00 P.M. that evening. He went from the boat straight to the home of Secretary of State William Seward, a few blocks from the White House. Seward, who had recently been badly injured in a carriage accident, lay still while Lincoln stretched across the foot of his bed and brought him encouraging news from the front and tales of his wondrous visit to Richmond. The president was happy. The war would be over soon. He could feel it. Lincoln and Seward did not yet know that, several hours ago, Lee had already surrendered.

After an hour of quiet talk, Lincoln went home. Crowds at the White House demanded that Lincoln show himself—the people had missed him and were disappointed that he had not been in Washington to celebrate the fall of Richmond with them. He stood at the second-floor window beneath the north portico and spoke a quick greeting. Later that night, news of Lee's surrender reached Washington. But no one knows what else Lincoln did after he heard the news. Was he too overjoyed to sleep that night? Did he walk the halls or go to his office and stare through the window into the night? Did he haunt the telegraph office? Did he know that tomorrow morning would begin the greatest day in the history of Washington?

The next morning, April 10, Abraham Lincoln, along with most of the city, awoke to the sound of gunfire. But the city wasn't under attack. A reporter described how the thunder of hundreds of guns let the citizens of Washington know of Lee's surrender. "Most people were sleeping soundly in their beds," he wrote, "when, at daylight on the rainy morning of April 10, 1865, a great boom startled the misty air of Washington, shaking the very earth, and breaking windows of houses about Lafayette Square. . . . Boom! Boom! went the guns, until five hundred were fired . . . for this was Secretary of War Stanton's way of telling the people that the Army of Northern Virginia had at last laid down its arms, and that peace had come again."

On this day of victory, no one in Washington was dwelling upon Jefferson Davis, his government in exile, or his last-ditch plans. There may still have been other Confederate armies in the field, but Lee had been the major threat. As far as the North was concerned, the war was over and the Union had won. For Abraham Lincoln it was the climax of the happiest week of his life. The whereabouts of the missing Confederate president and his officials were not front-page news. It was seven days after the fall of Richmond, and Lincoln had still not started a manhunt to capture Davis or the top Confederate leaders. He had his reasons.

CHAPTER FIVE

While Washington, D.C., began a week of rejoicing, word traveled to Danville. A messenger from Lee's army reached President Davis. The message he carried, said one of his officials, "fell upon the ears of all like a fire-bell in the night." The rider delivered his news to the president's office, where Jefferson Davis and several cabinet and staff members had gathered. Davis read the message, did not speak, and passed it on. Robert E. Lee had surrendered on April 9. The Army of Northern Virginia was no more. The war in Virginia was over. And Danville was in danger. The Confederate government had to get farther away from the Union armies by retreating at once, deeper into the Southern interior.

Leaving Danville meant not only fleeing a town but abandoning the state of Virginia. To Davis, this was a terrible blow. First he had lost his capital, Richmond; he had just lost his greatest general and his best army; and now he was about to lose all of Virginia. This series of three disasters, all in one week, made it much less likely that President Davis would be able to rally the people and save the nation.

The news devastated the president. He wondered whether it had been really necessary for Lee to surrender. Couldn't his best general have escaped from the Union army, headed south, and lived to fight another day? Davis feared that other Confederate generals would follow Lee's example. Such a chain of surrenders would be a catastrophe and would end the war once and for all.

Davis ordered his government to leave Danville by a night train to Greensboro, North Carolina. Burton Harrison, back at the president's side after escorting Varina Davis to safety in Charlotte, took control of the train. "We set to work at once to arrange for a railway train to convey the more important officers of the Government and such others as could be got aboard," he wrote. They also took "our luggage and as much material as it was desired to carry along, including the boxes and papers" that they had brought from Richmond.

The boxes were an important symbol. Despite the triple disasters of the week, the Confederate government would not leave Danville in a panic. It must maintain good order. As long as Davis kept his officials together and did not abandon the papers he needed to keep the government working, the Confederate States of America lived.

Many of the people in Danville hoped to get on the train and make their way farther south. Guards were posted to make sure that people who weren't supposed to be aboard could not get on. Dozens begged for passes that would let them ride the train. One general claimed that he possessed valuable fuses and explosives needed for the war, and Jefferson Davis told Harrison to find a place for the man and his daughters. Politely, Davis even offered to let one of the women share his seat.

One observer remembered what he saw as the train was loaded. It was dark and raining; the mud was knee-deep. Wagons were crowding, men were shouting, soldiers were cursing and trying to get past the guards. All of it, he said, "created a confusion such as it was never before the fortune of old Danville to witness."

At about eleven o'clock, the train finally moved off. "The night was intensely dark," one passenger remembered, "and with a slight rain, the road in wretched condition, and the progress was consequently very slow."

Soon Davis regretted offering to let the general's daughter sit beside him. She would not stop talking—discussing the weather, asking questions—unable to see that Davis was tired of her conversation. "There we all were," remembered Harrison, "in our seats, crowded together, waiting to be off, full of gloom at the situation, wondering what would happen next, and all as silent as mourners at a funeral; all except, indeed, the General's daughter, who prattled on in a voice everybody heard."

Then an explosion rocked the car. It had come from somewhere close to the president. No one knew what had just happened. Had Union troops intercepted the slow-moving train and opened fire on it or tossed a grenade into Davis's car? Or was it sabotage? Or had a traitor sitting in the car tried to murder the president with a suicide bomb?

Burton Harrison saw it all: "A sharp explosion occurred very near the President, and a young man was seen to bounce into the air, clapping both hands to the seat of his trowsers. We all sprang to our feet in alarm." The car smelled of black gunpowder. Harrison soon discovered that this was not an attack but an absurd accident. An officer, carrying fuses in the coattail pocket of his long frock coat, had sat down atop a stove. His weight crushed one of the fuses, setting off the explosion directly under his buttocks. Jefferson Davis and the others in the car were unharmed.

As the train went on its way toward Greensboro, North Carolina, Davis drafted a letter to the mayor of Danville, thanking him for taking the Confederate government in. "Sir," he wrote, "Permit me to return to yourself and council my sincere thanks for your kindness shown to me when I came among you." And he ended the letter, "May God bless and preserve you, and grant to our country independence and prosperity."

Davis still believed it was possible, with God's help, for the Confederacy to win the war and exist as an independent country. But when he would cross the state line the next day, April 11, he would have to accept the reality that Virginia, queen of the Confederacy, was lost.

While Jefferson Davis and the cabinet packed up in Danville, in Washington Abraham Lincoln enjoyed a spontaneous serenade outside his window. He made the crowd who had gathered on the White House lawn laugh by telling them that "Dixie" was one of the spoils of war and that he wanted to hear it played right now. Lincoln had loved the tune from the moment he first heard it. The band agreed, and the anthem of the Confederacy echoed through Lincoln's White House and drifted across the grounds and into the streets of the capital city of the Union.

Jefferson Davis's train arrived in Greensboro, North Carolina, at around 2:00 P.M. on April 11. His arrival horrified the citizens. Unlike in Danville, no people came forward to offer food and lodging to their president. The unfriendliness outraged Stephen Mallory, the secretary of the navy. He noted that there were many large and luxurious homes, "but their doors were closed and their 'latch-strings pulled in' against the members of the retreating government."

A colonel from Davis's staff invited the president to share his family's room, which he had rented for them after he had removed them from Richmond. But the owners of the house insisted that Davis must leave. They were terrified of what might happen to them if the Union armies learned that Jefferson Davis had stayed there. That fear was felt by most of the people of Greensboro. "It was rarely that anybody asked one of us to his house," Burton Harrison complained, "and but few of them even had the grace even to explain their fear that, if they entertained us, their houses would be burned by the enemy, when his **cavalry** should get there."

At last Davis and his officials were settled in what Stephen Mallory described as a "dilapidated, leaky" railroad passenger car. "Here they ate, slept, and lived during their stay in Greensboro," he wrote, "a negro boy cooking their rations in the open air near by." Just as they had made the best of their two train rides from Richmond and from Danville, the members of the Confederate government endured everything with good humor. The car became, said Mallory, "a very agreeable resort" during the "dreary days" in the unfriendly town. "The navy store supplied bread and bacon . . . biscuits, eggs, and coffee were added; and with a few tin cups, spoons, and pocket knives, and a liberal use of fingers and capital appetites, they managed to get enough to eat, and they slept as best they could." The highest officials of the Confederacy ate like common soldiers.

Mallory went on to describe how the Confederate officials managed their "curious life" in the train car. "Here was the astute 'Minister of Justice' . . . with a piece of half-broiled 'middling' in one hand and a hoe-cake in the other, his face bearing unmistakable evidence of the condition of the bacon. There was the clever Secretary of State busily dividing his attention between a bucket of stewed dried apples and a **haversack** of hard-boiled eggs. Here was the Postmaster-General sternly and energetically running his bowie knife through a ham as if it were the chief business of life, and there was the Secretary of the Navy courteously swallowing his coffee scalding hot that he might not keep the **venerable** Adjutant-General waiting too long for the **coveted** tin cup!"

A few days later Jefferson Davis would give a brief speech—no more than twelve or fifteen minutes long—in Greensboro. He boasted to his audience "how vast our resources still were, and that we would in a few weeks have a larger army than we ever had." Davis explained how such an army was to be raised. "Three fourths of the men are at home, absent without leave. Now we will collect them, and then there are a great many **conscripts** on the rolls who have never been caught—we will get them—and with the 100,000 men from Gen. Lee's army and the 85,000 men from Gen. Johnston's, we will have such an army as we have never had before."

But these remarks rested on wishful thinking. Lee's and Johnston's armies were much smaller than Davis imagined. Thousands of men had deserted and gone home, and Davis had no way to round them up and force them to fight. And even if, by some miracle, Jefferson Davis was able to assemble a force of 185,000 men or more, how would he arm them, feed them, and supply them with ammunition? And even if he could overcome these obstacles, the Union armies would still outnumber them.

★ ★ ★

On the afternoon of April 11, Abraham Lincoln sat in his office and wrote out a draft of an important speech he planned to deliver from the second-floor window of the White House that night. He did not know that he was preparing his last speech. He would honor the men who had won the war and then speak about giving blacks the right to vote.

On April 12 General Lee wrote to tell Davis what he already knew. This was Lee's official announcement to the president that he had surrendered.

Near Appomattox Court House, Virginia
April 12, 1865

Mr. President:

It is with pain that I announce to Your Excellency the surrender of the Army of Northern Virginia. . . . The enemy was more than five times our numbers. If we could have forced our way one day longer it would have been at a great sacrifice of life; at its end, I did not see how a surrender could have been avoided. We had no **subsistence** *for man or horse . . . the supplies could not reach us, and the men deprived of food and sleep for many days, were worn out and exhausted.*

With great respect, yr obdt svt [obedient servant]
R. E. Lee
Genl [General]

The arrival of General Lee's letter jolted President Davis into reality. Lee's son was there in Greensboro when Davis received it. "After reading it," the young man remembered, "he handed it without comment to us; then, turning away, he silently wept bitter tears."

At least the president's family was safe. Varina wrote to Jefferson on April 13, telling him she had crossed the North Carolina state line and was now in Chester, South Carolina. She kept traveling, hoping to avoid Union soldiers: "I am going somewhere, perhaps to Washington Ga—perhaps only to Abbeville just as the children seem to bear the journey I will decide. . . . I feel wordless, helpless—the children are well. . . . Would to God I could know the truth of the horrible rumors I hear of you. . . . May God have mercy upon me, and preserve you safe your devoted wife."

In Washington on April 13, Abraham Lincoln was busy. The war was not over. And when it was, he must plan the **reconstruction** of the South. He visited the telegraph office early in the morning and then had meetings with his generals and officials. At night the president, like all of Washington, enjoyed a grand **illumination** of the city to celebrate Lee's surrender.

The buildings of Washington glowed with candles, lamps, and decorations. One observer described what he saw: "The Capitol made a magnificent display—as did the whole city. After lighting up my own house and seeing the Capitol lighted, I rode up to the upper end of the City and saw the whole display. It was indeed glorious . . . *all of Washington* was in the streets. I never saw such a crowd out-of-doors in my life."

Not everyone in Washington enjoyed the illumination. In his room at the National Hotel at Pennsylvania Avenue and Sixth Street, the twenty-six-year-old actor John Wilkes Booth wrote a letter to his mother. "Everything was bright and splendid," he said. But, he lamented, "more so in my eyes if it had been a display in a nobler cause."

CHAPTER SIX

On April 14, Jefferson Davis sent a hurried note to Varina.

Greensboro N.C.
14 April 65

Dear Winnie

I will come to you if I can. Every thing is dark.—you should prepare for the worst by dividing your baggage so as to move in wagons. If you can go to Abbeville it seems best as I am now advised— If you can send every thing there do so—I have lingered on the road and labored to little purpose—My love to the children and Maggie— God bless and preserve you ever prays your most affectionate

Banny —

*I sent you a telegram but fear it was stopped on the road. Genl.
Bonham hears this and will [tell] you more than I can write as his
horse is at the door and he waits for me to write this again and
ever your's—*

Then he spent a quiet night wondering what events the coming
days might bring. His journey, although difficult, had not been a complete failure. Yes, he had fled Richmond, lost Lee and the Army of
Northern Virginia, and abandoned the state of Virginia to the enemy.
But the situation was not all bad. During his twelve days on the run, he
had escaped capture, kept his government together, and protected his
family. And he had kept his dignity. He had not fled Richmond like a
thief in the night, but as a head of state.

Abraham Lincoln began another busy day on April 14 with break-
fast with his son Robert, an army officer on Grant's staff and just back
from Lee's surrender. The president spent the day in meetings and writing letters. He agreed to go with his wife to Ford's Theatre that night to
see the comedy *Our American Cousin*. In the afternoon Abraham and
Mary Lincoln went on a carriage ride to the Navy Yard. He told her
that today he considered the war to be over. Abraham Lincoln wanted
to laugh tonight.

Around 8:30 P.M. the President and Mrs. Lincoln, along with their
companions, Major Henry Rathbone, an army officer, and his fiancée,
Clara Harris, daughter of a United States senator, got out of their carriage, walked several yards to the front door of Ford's Theatre, and
disappeared inside.

Abraham Lincoln loved the theater, and during the Civil War
he had gone to many plays. Tonight, while his parents attended *Our*

American Cousin, twelve-year-old Tad Lincoln enjoyed *Aladdin* at Grover's Theatre, a few blocks away. Lincoln's other son, twenty-one-year-old Robert, chose to stay at the White House to read.

At the Star Saloon, the brick building just south of Ford's, customers gulped their whiskeys and brandies and tossed their coins on the bar in payment. One of them—a handsome, pale-skinned, black-eyed, raven-haired young man with a mustache—swallowed his drink and left the bar without speaking a word. If anyone had been watching the front door of the Star Saloon between 9:30 and 10:00 P.M., he might have recognized John Wilkes Booth, one of the most famous stage stars in America, as he left wearing a black frock coat, black pants, thigh-high black leather riding boots, and a black hat.

Booth turned north up Tenth Street, saw the president's carriage parked several yards in front of him, and then turned right, toward the theater, passing through Ford's main door, the same one through which the president had entered about an hour earlier. If he intended to see the play, John Wilkes Booth was impossibly late.

It was ten o'clock. By eleven, quiet Tenth Street would be filled with a screaming mob of thousands of people.

It began between 10:15 and 10:30 P.M. At one moment the street was quiet. At the next dozens of playgoers rushed out the doors from Ford's Theatre onto Tenth Street. People pushed one another aside and knocked one another down to squeeze through the exits.

Some of the first men to escape the theater headed toward E and F Streets, shouting as they ran. Within seconds they turned the corners and vanished from sight. Then hundreds of men, women, and children fled Ford's and gathered in the street. Many screamed. Others wept. Soon their voices combined into a loud and fearful roar. They shouted strange words which pierced the din: "Murder." "Assassin." "President." "Dead."

Then random words formed into sentences: "Don't let him escape." "Catch him." "It was John Wilkes Booth!" "Burn the theater!" "The president has been shot." "President Lincoln is dead." "No, he's alive."

In the Petersen house, a boardinghouse across the street from Ford's Theatre, Henry Safford, who shared a second-floor rented room, heard the noise outside. He had not gone to bed and was still awake, reading a book. From his window he saw the crowd. Something was wrong. He raced downstairs, unlocked the door, and hurried into the street. He pushed through the crowd. Halfway across, the mob blocked his progress. He could not take another step. There were too many people. He saw that this crowd was angry, perhaps dangerous. But why?

Safford decided to return to the safety of the Petersen house. "Finding it impossible to go further, as everyone acted crazy or mad, I retreated to the steps of my house," he wrote later. Before he got out of the mob, he heard its news: Abraham Lincoln had just been assassinated in Ford's Theatre. He had been shot, the murderer had escaped, and the president was still inside.

Other boarders at Petersen's heard the noise outside. George Francis and his wife, Huldah, lived on the first floor, and their two big front parlor windows faced the theater. "We were about getting into bed," Francis recalled. "Huldah had got into bed. I had changed my clothes and shut off the gas, when we heard such a terrible scream that we ran to the front window to see what it could mean." Looking out into the street, they saw "a great commotion—in the Theatre—some running in, others hurrying out, and we could hear hundreds of voices mingled in the greatest confusion. Presently we heard some one say 'the

President is shot,' when I hurried on my clothes and ran out, across the street, as they brought him out of the Theatre—Poor man! I could see as the gas light fell upon his face, that it was deathly pale, and that his eyes were closed."

While George Francis stayed in the street, Henry Safford had returned to the Petersen house. From the first-floor porch, he noticed a commotion at one of the theater doors, and then watched a small knot of people push their way into the street. An army officer waved his sword in the air, bellowing at people to step back and clear the way. Someone else ran from Ford's across the street and pounded on the door of the house next to the Petersen house. No one answered.

In command of that little group was Dr. Charles A. Leale, a U.S. army surgeon who had been watching the play and who was the first doctor to see Lincoln after the shooting. "When we arrived to the street," he remembered, "I was asked to place him in a carriage and remove him to the White House. This I refused to do fearing that he would die as soon as he would be placed in an upright position. I said that I wished to take him to the nearest house, and, place him comfortably in bed. We slowly crossed the street."

Safford watched the little group of several men inch through the mob. They were carrying something. It was a man. It was the body of Abraham Lincoln. "Where can we take him?" Safford heard one of the men shout.

Henry Safford seized a candle and held it up so that the men carrying the president could see it. "Bring him in here!" he yelled. He waved the light. "Bring him in here!" He caught their attention. "I saw a man," said Dr. Leale, "standing at the door of Mr. Petersen's house holding a candle in his hand and beckoning us to enter."

Lincoln's bearers walked from Ford's Theatre to the Petersen house.

The Petersen House, where Lincoln died.

From the safety of her front parlor, Huldah Francis watched them get closer and closer. Soon they were right below her window. When she saw the men carrying Lincoln up the steps, she hurried to put on her clothes. George Francis raced back to the house to join his wife.

Henry Safford invited the men inside. "Take us to your best room," Dr. Leale commanded. Safford led Dr. Leale and the men carrying Lincoln into the front hall. On the right, a narrow staircase led up to the second floor. On the left was a closed door.

Leale had asked for the "best room." That would be the one where George and Huldah Francis lived. Safford took the handle of the door to their parlor and turned it. Locked! Safford headed deeper into the dim hallway and stopped at a second door on the left, the one to the Francises' bedroom. Also locked! Behind that door, Huldah Francis was dressing.

There was just one room left, the smallest one on the first floor. Safford turned the doorknob. It was unlocked. And the room was empty. The boarder, Private William Clarke, had gone out for the evening to celebrate the end of the war.

It was enough for Leale. He ordered the bearers to carry Lincoln into the room and lay him on the bed.

A few minutes later Mary Lincoln appeared in the doorway of the Petersen house. Major Rathbone and Clara Harris had helped her through the wailing mob in the street and into the house. George Francis saw her arrival. "She was perfectly frantic," he remembered. "'Where is my husband! Where is my husband!' she cried, wringing her hands." Moments later she reached the back room, where she found Lincoln lying on a bed. Dr. Leale and two other doctors, who had also been in the audience at Ford's, were bent over Lincoln. George Francis watched as Mary saw her husband. "As she approached his bedside she bent over him, kissing him again and again, exclaiming 'How can it be so? Do speak to me!'"

Leale asked Mary to go into the next room while the doctors examined her husband. She agreed. Henry Rathbone and Clara Harris brought Mary to the front parlor and seated her on a large sofa. Rathbone felt light-headed. Moments after John Wilkes Booth shot the president, the actor had stabbed Rathbone in the arm. The wound was deep, and the cut would not stop bleeding. He sat down in the hall and then fainted. When he awoke later, he was picked up from the floor and delivered to his house. He would live.

The doctors dragged William Clarke's bed away from the walls so that they could see Lincoln better. Then they pushed all the chairs close to the bed. Leale ordered everyone except the two other doctors to leave the room. They stripped their patient and searched his body for other wounds.

In the front parlor Mary Lincoln was coming apart. When Clara Harris sat beside her on the sofa and tried to comfort her, Mary could not take her eyes off Clara's bloodstained dress: "My husband's blood!" she cried. "My husband's blood." The First Lady did not know that it was Henry Rathbone's blood, not the president's, on Clara's dress. If Mary had examined her own dress, she would have been horrified, for it did bear the stains of her husband's blood.

Mary Lincoln needed help. Clara Harris would not do—Mary hardly knew her. The First Lady had few friends in Washington, and now she asked for them all: Mary Jane Welles, wife of navy secretary Gideon Welles; Elizabeth Keckly, her black dressmaker; and Elizabeth Dixon, wife of a United States senator. Messengers ran off in search of the women. While she waited for her friends to arrive at her side, Mary, in torment, sat on the sofa. The crowd was just outside the windows.

She could hear their voices.

Elizabeth Dixon was the first of Mary's friends to arrive. She saw a gruesome scene that horrified her: "On a common bedstead covered with an army blanket and a colored woolen coverlid lay stretched the murdered President his life blood slowly ebbing away," she remembered. "The officers of the government were there & no lady except Miss Harris whose dress was spattered with blood as was Mrs. Lincoln's who was frantic with grief calling him to take her with him, to speak one word to her. . . . I held and supported her as well as I could & twice we persuaded her to go into another room."

Throughout the night Dr. Leale watched Mary Lincoln stagger from the front parlor into the bedroom. "Mrs. Lincoln accompanied by Mrs. Senator Dixon came into the room several times during the course of the night. Mrs. Lincoln at one time exclaiming, 'Oh, that my Taddy might see his Father before he died' and then she fainted and was carried from the room."

Tad was not at the Petersen house with his grieving mother and his dying father. Earlier one of the men who had rushed out of Ford's had run to nearby Grover's Theatre. Someone from the audience remembered what happened next. "Miss German had just finished a song called 'Sherman's March Down to the Sea' and was about to repeat it," he recalled, "when the door of the theatre was pushed violently open and a man rushed in exclaiming 'turn out for Gods sake, the President has been shot in his private box at Ford's Theatre.'" The theater manager also announced the news from the stage. This was how Tad Lincoln, watching the play, learned that his father had been shot.

Tad was brought not to the Petersen house but to the White House by the doorkeeper. By the time he got home, his older brother, Robert

Lincoln, had already left to join his parents. Without his mother or older brother to comfort Tad, or even explain to him what had happened to his father, the frightened boy spent the night with servants in the near-empty mansion.

Shortly after 8:00 A.M. the next morning, Mary and Robert returned to the White House and informed Tad that his beloved "Pa" was dead. Tad felt again the fear and pain that he had suffered three years before when his brother Willie had died. During the long night, not once had Robert or Mary Lincoln gone to Tad. Nor had they ordered a messenger to bring him to the Petersen house and his dying father. It was the first troubling sign of how, in the days to come, Mary Lincoln's grief caused her to neglect her miserable and lonely little boy.

While Tad stayed alone at the White House through the night of April 14, Leale and the other doctors examined the president. More doctors arrived soon. But nothing could save Lincoln. By midnight it had become a death watch. All they would do now was observe and wait.

A second assassin had struck in Washington the night of April 14. At 10:15 P.M., about the same time that John Wilkes Booth shot the president, another assailant had invaded the home of the secretary of state. William Seward, bedridden from a carriage accident, lay in his bed. The attacker stabbed and slashed him almost to death; wounded an army sergeant serving as Seward's nurse; and stabbed a State Department messenger. He also struck Seward's son with a pistol, crushing his victim's skull and leaving him unconscious.

Runners carried the news of the attack on Seward to Secretary of War Edwin M. Stanton and Secretary of the Navy Gideon Welles, who were at their homes preparing for bed. Neither had yet heard about the assassination of the president. Each man raced by carriage to Seward's mansion. There they first heard rumors of another attack, this one upon the president at Ford's Theatre. Together Stanton and Welles drove a carriage to Tenth Street and arrived at the Petersen house before midnight.

Stanton barreled his way though the crowded hallway. He knew quickly that Lincoln was a dead man. There was nothing he could do for him. Except work. There was much to do. Stanton prepared himself for the long night ahead. He would lead the investigation of the crime, interview witnesses, send telegrams, launch the manhunt for Booth and his accomplices, and take precautions to prevent more assassinations.

As news of the assassination spread through Washington, many important public officials hurried to the Petersen house. Some came and went. Others stayed, sometimes for hours. Welles decided that at least one person should remain by Abraham Lincoln's side until the end. He volunteered. And he would record in his diary what he saw. Lincoln was stretched out "diagonally across the bed, which was not long enough for him. He had been stripped of his clothes. His large arms were of a size which one would scarce have expected from his spare form. His features were calm and striking. I have never seen them appear to better advantage, than for the first hour I was there. The room was small and overcrowded. The surgeons and members of the Cabinet were as many as should have been in the room, but there were many more, and the hall and other rooms in front were full."

Welles remembered that Lincoln, earlier that day, had told of a dream he'd had. In the dream Lincoln found himself aboard a ship

The Petersen House deathbed vigil,
sketched by an artist from the Army Medical Museum.

sailing rapidly toward shore. The president said that he'd had this vision before many great battles of the Civil War. Had a warning of his own assassination come to Abraham Lincoln in the night? As Gideon Welles sat beside his dying leader, he did not know that, several days earlier, Lincoln had dreamed a far more vivid nightmare of death.

A few days before the assassination, the president, Mary Lincoln, and two or three friends were gathered. One observed that Lincoln was in a "melancholy, meditative mood." The president had talked about the meaning of dreams. Mary asked her husband if he believed in dreams. "'I can't say that I do,'" he replied, "'but I had one the other night which has haunted me ever since.'" Lincoln told what his dream had been.

"'There seemed to be a death-like stillness about me. Then I heard . . . sobs, as if a number of people were weeping. I thought I left my bed and wandered downstairs. There the silence was broken by the same pitiful sobbing, but the mourners were invisible. I went from room to room; no living person was in sight. . . . It was light in all the rooms; every object was familiar to me; but where were all the people who were grieving as if their hearts would break? I was puzzled and alarmed. What could be the meaning of all this? . . . I kept on until I arrived at the East Room, which I entered. There I met with a sickening surprise. Before me was a catafalque [a platform], on which rested a corpse. . . . Around it were soldiers who were acting as guards. . . . 'Who is dead in the White House?' I demanded of one of the soldiers. 'The President,' was his answer; 'he was killed by an assassin!' Then came a loud burst of grief from the crowd, which awoke me from my dream. I slept no more than night . . ."

Mary Lincoln recoiled. "'That is horrid! I wish you had not told it.

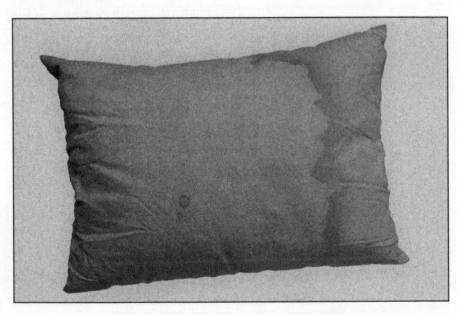

Bloody relic: a pillow from Lincoln's deathbed.

I am glad that I don't believe in dreams, or I should be in terror from this time forth.'"

"'Well,'" replied the president, "'it is only a dream, Mary. Let us say no more about it, and try to forget it.'"

Now Lincoln's nightmare had come true.

CHAPTER SEVEN

The news of the attacks on Lincoln and Seward stunned Washington. Crowds from all over the city came to stand outside the Petersen house, and many tried to enter but were turned back by soldiers guarding the door. One person who was allowed inside was Benjamin Brown French, commissioner of public buildings and grounds. He was in charge of all of the major public buildings in Washington. If Lincoln died, he would have much to do in the next few days. It would be his responsibility to decorate the city with the symbols of mourning.

French had slept through the night and had not heard about Lincoln's murder until the morning of April 15. When he woke, he saw that the streetlamps were still burning, although it was daylight. "I lay awake, perhaps ½ an hour," he remembered, "& seeing that they were still burning, I arose and saw a sentry passing before my house. I thought something wrong had happened, so dressed & went down & opened the front door."

A soldier came along and said, "Are not the doings of last night dreadful?" French asked what he meant by that. The soldier replied, "Have you not heard?" and told French that the president had been shot in Ford's Theatre "and Secretary Seward's throat cut in his residence." French ordered the Capitol building closed and hurried to the Petersen house. There he found Lincoln, who was still alive, in the back bedroom. As he hovered over the deathbed in the crowded little bedroom, perhaps he already wondered: Where, in all of Washington, could he hope to find enough black mourning **crepe** and bunting?

Early on April 15 Dr. Leale knew that Lincoln would not live long: "As morning dawned it became quite evident that he was gradually

THE PRESIDENT IS DEAD!

WAR DEPARTMENT,
Washington, April 15, 1865.

To MAJ. GEN. DIX,
Abraham Lincoln died this morning at 22 minutes after Seven o'clock.
E. M. STANTON, Sec. of War.

An early broadside announcing Lincoln's death.

sinking," he remembered. It was past 6:00 A.M. when Mary Lincoln returned to the bedroom. One of the doctors there recalled the scene. Mary fell in a faint, and when she awoke, she was taken to the bed to speak to her dying husband. "'Love,' she exclaimed, 'live but one moment to speak to me once—to speak to our children.'"

As Lincoln's breathing became louder and more labored, Mary cried out with fear and again fell fainting to the floor. Edwin Stanton heard her and came in from the room next door. He ordered, "Take that woman out and do not let her in again." He was obeyed. Mary Lincoln never saw her husband alive again.

At 7:22 A.M. on April 15, Abraham Lincoln died.

But what had begun in the little back room of a boardinghouse

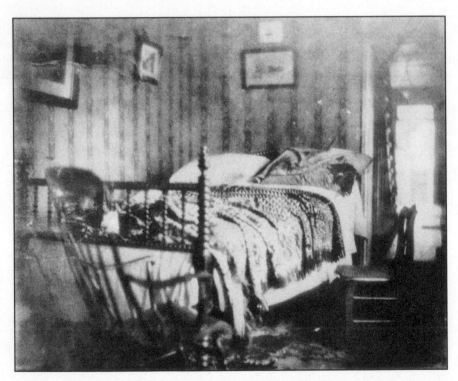

The bloody death bed shortly after Lincoln's body was removed.

in downtown Washington would not end with Lincoln's death. Soon the assassination would set in motion strong forces, the likes of which America had never seen. In the days to come, millions of Americans would join the procession that had begun that night when a handful of their fellow citizens made a pilgrimage to look upon their dying president.

Jefferson Davis awoke on the morning of April 15 not knowing anything about what had taken place in Washington. Davis did not know John Wilkes Booth, and had not sent him to kill Lincoln. Nor did Davis know that Booth was on the run, the prey of what would soon become a nationwide manhunt. He had no idea that within hours his longtime archenemy, Vice President Andrew Johnson, would succeed Lincoln as president. Johnson was a hardened foe of Southern plantation owners. The South could expect no mercy from him.

Worse, this morning's newspapers accused Davis himself of being the mastermind behind the great crime. Many demanded Davis's death by hanging or horrible torture. But Jefferson Davis was in the dark. For several days he would not know that Abraham Lincoln was dead.

Davis left Greensboro on April 15. Secretary of the Navy Mallory encouraged the president to not just get out of Greensboro, but to flee the country. There was no more hope of a military victory, Mallory believed. Davis should make himself "ready to cross the Mississippi and get into Mexico, or to leave the coast of Florida for the Bahamas or Cuba."

But Mallory could see that Jefferson Davis had no intention of leaving the country as long as there were any soldiers willing to fight for his cause. If his staff had known that Lincoln had just been murdered, they might have demanded that Davis flee to escape the North's vengeance. But they did not know, and so they packed up for the next stage of their journey south.

There were no trains at Greensboro, so Davis's party switched to horses, wagons, and carts. They left Greensboro on horseback on the afternoon of April 15. Burton Harrison wrote that the roads were hard to travel on: "Heavy rains had recently fallen. . . . The soil was a sticky red clay, the mud was awful."

On the morning of April 15, what thoughts must have raced through Edwin Stanton's mind as he left the Petersen house? He kept no diary, so we do not know exactly what he was thinking. But there were questions that must have weighed heavily on him. Where were the assassins? Would there be more attacks? And what about Lincoln's funeral? There must be one. But Stanton had no time to plan it. He must find someone to take over this important task. But who? And where would the president be buried? And the Union must still win the war.

But first it was time to bring Abraham Lincoln home to the White House. Lincoln's body had been placed in a plain wooden box. Soldiers carried it into the street and placed it in a horse-drawn hearse. All of the soldiers in the procession, even the officers, walked rather than rode their horses. They removed their hats and marched bareheaded. It was a sign of respect for their fallen commander. There was no band, no drums. The officers set the pace with the thud of their own steps on the dirt street. It would be the first of three Lincoln death processions in Washington.

One observer remembered looking out the window to watch Lincoln's body pass by. "I stepped to the window and saw the coffin of the dead President being placed in the hearse which passed up Tenth street to F and thus to the White House. . . . My hand involuntarily went to my head in salute as they started on their long, long journey back to the prairies and the hearts he knew and loved so well, the mortal remains of the greatest American of all time."

A newspaper reporter, wandering the streets, met the funeral procession on its way. "Wandering aimlessly up F Street toward Ford's Theater," he wrote, "we met a tragical procession. It was headed by a group of army officers walking bareheaded, and behind them, carried tenderly by a company of soldiers, was the **bier** of the dead President, covered with the flag of the Union, and accompanied by an escort of soldiers who had been on duty at the house where Lincoln died. . . . Every head was uncovered, and profound silence which prevailed was broken only by sobs and by the sound of the measured tread of those who bore the martyred President back to the home which he had so lately quitted full of life, hope, and cheer."

Arriving at the White House, the soldiers carried the temporary coffin into the Guest Room. They removed the flag that draped the box and then unscrewed the lid. They lifted the body and laid it on boards supported by wood sawhorses. They unwrapped the bloody flag from around Lincoln's body. At the Petersen house, his clothes—suit coat, torn shirt, pants, plus the contents of his pockets—had been tossed in the box. Somebody had forgotten his boots; they were still under Willie Clarke's bed. His tie was missing— somebody had already taken it. Abraham Lincoln lay naked on the boards. He had been dead for fewer than five hours. His body was still cooling.

Several doctors were waiting to perform an autopsy—an examination of Lincoln's dead body. They prepared their instruments. Dr. Janvier Woodward would expose the brain. He took a scalpel, sliced through the skin at the back of the president's head, and peeled the scalp forward to expose the skull. Then he reached for the bone saw. To get to the brain, he needed to cut off the top of Lincoln's skull.

This was done. They looked for the bullet but did not find it at first. Then Dr. Charles Crane, the assistant surgeon general, lifted the brain out of the skull. He described what happened next. "Suddenly the bullet dropped out through my fingers and fell, breaking the solemn silence of the room with its clatter, into an empty basin that was standing beneath. There it lay upon the white china, a little black mass no bigger than the end of my finger—dull, motionless and harmless, yet the cause of such mighty changes in the world's history as we may perhaps never realize." The bullet that had killed Abraham Lincoln was sent to the Army Medical Museum.

The bullet that ended Lincoln's life.

THE "BULLET," WITH WHICH OUR MARTYR PRESIDENT A. LINCOLN WAS ASSASSINATED BY J. W. BOOTH, AS SEEN UNDER A MICROSCOPE.

A bizarre print depicting Booth imprisoned inside his own bullet.

During the autopsy a messenger from the First Lady arrived to ask for a lock of Lincoln's hair as a memento. One of the doctors clipped off enough hair to send some to Mary Lincoln and to give pieces to all the doctors in the room.

Another doctor suggested weighing Lincoln's brain. Perhaps his brain was larger than that of ordinary people—that might account for his genius. But it turned out that it was of ordinary weight for a man of his size. The secret of his intelligence was not in the weight of his brain.

Their work done, the doctors wiped their tools clean and packed their instruments away. The president's body looked ghastly. The skin

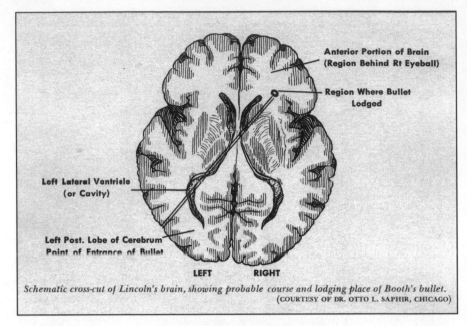

Anterior Portion of Brain
(Region Behind Rt Eyeball)

Region Where Bullet
Lodged

Left Lateral Ventricle
(or Cavity)

Left Post. Lobe of Cerebrum
Point of Entrance of Bullet

LEFT   RIGHT

Schematic cross-cut of Lincoln's brain, showing probable course and lodging place of Booth's bullet.
(COURTESY OF DR. OTTO L. SAPHIR, CHICAGO)

The bullet's fatal path.

was pale, the jaw slack, the eyelids slightly open, the face bruised, the scalp peeled back, the top of the skull sawn off, and the brain lying nearby in a basin. The **embalmers** arrived. It was their job to repair, or at least hide, the damage. The body was drained of blood, parts that would decay quickly were removed, and it was injected with chemicals that caused it to turn as solid and hard as a statue.

Edwin Stanton went through Lincoln's wardrobe to choose the suit he would be buried in. Abraham Lincoln had never cared much about his clothes; he usually wore whatever he owned until it was worn out. But Stanton did find one new black suit that he thought would do. He watched as the embalmers fitted the president with a white cotton shirt, attached a black bow tie under his collar, and dressed him in the clothes Stanton had chosen.

Lincoln's corpse was ready for his funeral. But Edwin Stanton had no time to organize it. He would have to choose someone else to set in motion Washington's grand farewell to Abraham Lincoln.

Stanton picked George Harrington, assistant secretary of the treasury. Harrington would take charge of all events in Washington honoring the late president. But at the moment there were no events to take charge of. No American president had ever been murdered. It would be up to Harrington to figure out how the capital should pay tribute to its first assassinated president.

Now that Lincoln's body was prepared for burial, a few visitors were allowed to pass into the White House, climb the stairs, enter the dark chamber, and view the body. Only relatives, close friends, and high officials were given permission. Mary Lincoln's friend and dressmaker Elizabeth Keckly was one of them.

After the president had been shot, Mary had sent a messenger summoning Keckly to her side. She had rushed to the White House, but guards would not let the free black woman enter. Keckly did not see Mary until the next day.

"I shall never forget the scene," Keckly wrote afterward, "the wails of a broken heart, the unearthly shrieks." She worried about Tad. He was silent in his own grief and frightened by his mother's outbursts. "Sometimes he would throw his arms around her neck," she described, "and exclaim, between his broken sobs, 'Don't cry so, Momma! Don't cry, or you will make me cry too! You will break my heart.'"

Keckly comforted Mary and then asked to see Abraham Lincoln. "[Mrs. Lincoln] was nearly exhausted with grief, and when she became a little quiet, I received permission to go into the Guest Room, where the body of the President lay in state," she wrote. "When I crossed the threshold of the room I could not help recalling the day on which I had seen little Willie [Lincoln] lying in his coffin where the body of his father now lay. I remembered how the president had wept over the pale beautiful face of his gifted boy, and now the President himself was dead."

Strangely, Mary Lincoln did not make a private visit to her husband. Her last nightmare vision of him as he lay dying was too terrible. She could not bear to walk the short distance from her bedchamber to the Guest Room and look upon his face now. Tad stayed in her bedchamber with her. We don't know whether Tad's older brother, Robert, took the younger boy to the Guest Room to view their father, just as, three years before, Abraham had carried Tad from his bed to view his brother Willie in death.

For three days and two nights, Lincoln's body rested on a table in the White House. Except for a few visitors and the guards standing around his corpse, he was alone. The only sounds in the house were those Lincoln would have remembered from childhood—wood saws cutting, hammers pounding nails, carpenters at work. Workmen in the East Room were building the platform upon which his elaborate coffin, not yet finished, would soon rest, and were building the benches upon which the funeralgoers would sit.

Outside this room, the nation was in upheaval. The assassin John Wilkes Booth had escaped, and Secretary of War Edwin Stanton was directing the manhunt to capture him. Stanton worried that there might be other assassins, perhaps plotting attacks on the highest officials of Lincoln's government. Stanton ordered every one of them protected by a military guard around the clock.

And Confederate president Jefferson Davis was unaccounted for. Stanton thought that Davis planned to rally the South to fight on. Many newspaper stories in the North suggested that Lincoln's murder was part of Davis's plan to win the war. Even if that wasn't true, there was still danger from Confederate troops. Lee had surrendered, but he did not command the Confederacy's only army. There were still other armies in the field ready to fight.

As Stanton worked and worried, George Harrington labored long hours to organize the grandest funeral ceremony in American history. This was his plan:

On Tuesday, April 18, the public would be able to come to the East Room of the White House and view the president's body.

On Wednesday, April 19, there would be a funeral, and then a procession to carry Abraham Lincoln's body to the Capitol.

On Friday, April 21, another funeral procession would take the body to the train station, where it would be taken to the place he would be buried.

Many questions remained unsettled. For how many hours should the White House be kept open for the public to view the remains? How many people per hour could squeeze through the doors? Who should be invited to the funeral? And where could it be held? The East Room was the biggest room in the White House, but it could never hold everyone who would want to say a last farewell to Lincoln. And where would they find enough chairs for all of them? George Harrington needed help.

He called a meeting of several of the most important army officers in Washington. They had much work to do and little time—just sixty-eight hours to plan Abraham Lincoln's funeral.

Harrington's duties would end once the ceremonies in Washington were over. Secretary of War Edwin Stanton had taken responsibility for the next stage of the president's journey.

But one important question remained. Where would Abraham Lincoln be buried? In Washington? Under the United States Capitol, in an empty crypt once intended for but never occupied by George Washington's body? Or would Mary Lincoln take the body home to Illinois? Would he be laid to rest in Chicago, its most important city, or in Springfield, Lincoln's home for the past twenty-four years? What about Kentucky, where he had been born? It was up to Mary Lincoln to decide. At last she and her son Robert settled on Springfield.

Now the secretary of war was able to plan the route of the train that would carry Lincoln's body. That train *could* head for Illinois by the shortest and most direct route. But that might not be best. Four years earlier, in 1861, after Abraham Lincoln had been elected president of the United States, he had taken a long train trip through several of the major Northern states. He wanted to see the American people and let them see him. He gave speeches, greeted important officials, mingled with ordinary citizens, and took part in ceremonies. For Abraham Lincoln that journey was a symbol of the bond between himself and the American people.

Now he was dead. In their grief, Americans had not forgotten the train ride of 1861. At the War Department telegrams began to pour in from the cities and towns that had seen him on his journey east from the prairie four years ago. Send him back to us, they asked. Edwin Stanton liked the idea. The assassination of President Lincoln was a national tragedy. But the American people could not come from all over the country to view the president's body, attend the funeral, or march in the procession. Then why couldn't Abraham Lincoln go to them?

It could be done. There was only one thing in the way—the president's widow. First Mary Lincoln would have to agree.

Stanton talked to her. Might she, he asked, consider soothing the grief of the American people by agreeing to send his body by train through the great cities of the Union? From Washington the train would head to Maryland, Pennsylvania, New Jersey, and New York, then make the great turn west, passing through Ohio and Indiana and into northern Illinois, then make a final turn south from Chicago, down through the prairies and home to Springfield.

There was one more thing. The people wanted to see their Father Abraham, not just his closed coffin. They wanted to look upon his face. That meant his coffin would have to be open for a journey of more than sixteen hundred miles. To Mary Lincoln the idea seemed ghoulish. The idea of exhibiting her dear husband's remains for all to see horrified her. But at the same time, she liked thinking of a grand funeral pageant that would show what a great man Lincoln had been. She said yes.

CHAPTER EIGHT

At the Treasury Department George Harrington began adding up the number of people who had to receive an invitation to the White House funeral. Letters and telegrams begging for tickets to the funeral or positions in the procession poured in. While Harrington worked and planned, Abraham Lincoln spent his last night in the White House.

Two days after the president died, the coffin was ready. Soldiers carried it to the second-floor Guest Room and placed it on the floor. They lifted the president's body from the table where he had lain since Saturday afternoon. The

George Harrington, the man who planned all Lincoln funeral events in Washington.

soldiers carried him to the coffin—it looked too small. How would they fit him into it? Abraham Lincoln was six feet, four inches tall, and the coffin turned out to be just two inches taller. It was a snug fit. If they had tried to bury him in his boots, he would have been too tall.

The soldiers lifted the coffin and carried it down the stairs. They took it to the center of the East Room and rested it upon a platform. The coffin itself was expensive and magnificent, probably not what Lincoln would have chosen for himself. Why, it had cost almost as much as he paid for his house in Springfield.

Lincoln's body lay waiting in the East Room for his funeral. It would not be the first funeral of someone from the Lincoln family in the White House. Three years earlier, Lincoln had attended the funeral of his son Willie. It was, he said, "the hardest trial of my life."

William Wallace Lincoln, age eleven, was the president's favorite son. Tall and thin, Willie looked like his father. His mind worked, Abraham said, in ways that reminded him of himself. Willie was his father's true companion in the White House and the favorite of many of those who lived and worked there. Lincoln loved no one more.

In February 1862 both Tad and Willie fell ill with a fever. They got worse, and the president watched over them with a keen eye. During the next two weeks, they became seriously ill. The *Evening Star* began printing reports on how they were doing. On February 20 the newspaper wrote, "BETTER.—We are glad to say that the President's second son—Willie—who has been so dangerously ill seems better to-day."

But this last report was wrong. Willie Lincoln died the afternoon of February 20, at 5:00 P.M. Lincoln cried out to his secretary, "My boy is gone—he is actually gone!" Willie, he said, "was too good for this earth . . . but then we loved him so. It is hard, hard to have him die!"

Willie's body was laid out in the Green Room of the White House as arrangements were made for his funeral. While the boy's body lay a short distance away, a man looking for a government job made the mistake of bothering Abraham Lincoln. Lincoln had made it a lifelong habit to control his temper, and it was a rare thing when he showed anger in public. But if pushed too far, Lincoln would sometimes unleash his wrath—as he did at this unwelcome visitor.

"When you came to the door here, didn't you see the crepe on it?" he demanded. "Didn't you realize that meant somebody must be lying dead in this house?"

"Yes, Mr. Lincoln, I did. But what I wanted to see you about was very important."

"That crepe is hanging there for my son; his dead body at this moment is lying unburied in this house, and you come here, push yourself in with such a request! Couldn't you at least have the decency to wait until after we had buried him?"

On February 23 friends and family viewed Willie's body at the White House. On February 24, the day of Willie's funeral, the government offices were closed, as if an important politician had died. Leaders of the government, members of Congress, officers from the army, and other important people from all over Washington came to his funeral.

The *Evening Star* published a heartbreaking description of the scene: "His remains were placed in the Green room . . . where this morning a great many friends of the family called to take a last look at the little favorite, who had endeared himself to all guests of the family.

e body was clothed in the usual every-day attire of youths of his age, sisting of pants and jacket with white stockings and low shoes—the ite collar and wristbands being turned over the black cloth of the ket."

Willie's coffin was very plain. It had a square silver plate with a few ple words:

William Wallace Lincoln.
Born December 21st, 1850.
Died February 20th, 1862.

fter the funeral Willie's body was carried to Oak Hill Cemetery rby Georgetown. There it was placed in a tomb until the day Abraham Lincoln could take him home to Illinois.

coln prayed that Tad, still sick, would be spared. On February *Evening Star* reported that he would live: "We are glad to learn youngest son of the President is still improving in health, and nsidered entirely out of danger."

ham and Mary Lincoln mourned Willie in different ways. away anything that could remind her of her dead son. She ll of his toys and would not allow his friends to come to House to play with Tad. The sight of them, she said, upset . Instead, Mary found relief in the world of dreams and she imagined she saw Willie, along with her other son ad died many years ago, and her half brother, Alec, who uncle. "He comes to me every night," she swore to her comes to me . . . and stands at the foot of my bed with the t, adorable smile he has always had; he does not always come

alone; little Eddie is sometimes with him and twice he has come v
our brother Alec, he tells me he loves his Uncle Alec and is with h
most of the time. You cannot dream of the comfort this gives me."

Abraham Lincoln saw his son in his memory. Willie died or
Thursday, and every Thursday for several weeks the president lock
himself in his office for a time to mourn and to think of his son. I
one dared to interrupt him. And at night he dreamed of his lost bo

Death also visited Jefferson Davis's White House. On the aftern
of Saturday, April 30, 1864, an officer walking near the Confed
White House saw a crying young girl run out of the mansion and
violently on the bell cord of the next house. Then another gi
boy fled the White House. A black female servant who followec
told the officer that one of the Davis children was badly hui
officer ran inside and found a male servant holding in his arms
boy, "insensible and almost dead." It was five-year-old Josep
Davis. His brother, Jeff Jr., was kneeling beside him, trying
him speak. "I have said all the prayers I know," said Jeff, "but
not wake Joe." Jefferson and Varina were not home.

Joseph had fallen fifteen feet from a porch. He was fo
on the brick pavement, unconscious, with a broken left
a severely contused forehead. His chest evidenced signs
injuries. The officer sent for a doctor and then began to
with camphor and brandy, and applied a mustard or
wrists. The child, he observed, "had beautiful black e
and was a very handsome boy." The treatment, wrote th
a letter a few days after the event, seemed to work: "In a
he began to breathe better, and opened his eyes, and we a
he was revived, but it was the last bright gleaming of the wic

ne
n

nea
n a
Lin
the
the
ow co
Abral
y sent
w out
White h
too much
ts, where
ie, who h
Willie's
"He
swee

The body was clothed in the usual every-day attire of youths of his age, consisting of pants and jacket with white stockings and low shoes—the white collar and wristbands being turned over the black cloth of the jacket."

Willie's coffin was very plain. It had a square silver plate with a few simple words:

William Wallace Lincoln.
Born December 21st, 1850.
Died February 20th, 1862.

After the funeral Willie's body was carried to Oak Hill Cemetery in nearby Georgetown. There it was placed in a tomb until the day when Abraham Lincoln could take him home to Illinois.

Lincoln prayed that Tad, still sick, would be spared. On February 26 the *Evening Star* reported that he would live: "We are glad to learn that the youngest son of the President is still improving in health, and is now considered entirely out of danger."

Abraham and Mary Lincoln mourned Willie in different ways. Mary sent away anything that could remind her of her dead son. She threw out all of his toys and would not allow his friends to come to the White House to play with Tad. The sight of them, she said, upset her too much. Instead, Mary found relief in the world of dreams and spirits, where she imagined she saw Willie, along with her other son Eddie, who had died many years ago, and her half brother, Alec, who was Willie's uncle. "He comes to me every night," she swore to her sister. "He comes to me . . . and stands at the foot of my bed with the same sweet, adorable smile he has always had; he does not always come alone; little Eddie is sometimes with him and twice he has come with our brother Alec, he tells me he loves his Uncle Alec and is with him most of the time. You cannot dream of the comfort this gives me."

Abraham Lincoln saw his son in his memory. Willie died on a Thursday, and every Thursday for several weeks the president locked himself in his office for a time to mourn and to think of his son. No one dared to interrupt him. And at night he dreamed of his lost boy.

Death also visited Jefferson Davis's White House. On the afternoon of Saturday, April 30, 1864, an officer walking near the Confederate White House saw a crying young girl run out of the mansion and yank violently on the bell cord of the next house. Then another girl and boy fled the White House. A black female servant who followed them told the officer that one of the Davis children was badly hurt. The officer ran inside and found a male servant holding in his arms a little boy, "insensible and almost dead." It was five-year-old Joseph Evan Davis. His brother, Jeff Jr., was kneeling beside him, trying to make him speak. "I have said all the prayers I know," said Jeff, "but God will not wake Joe." Jefferson and Varina were not home.

Joseph had fallen fifteen feet from a porch. He was found lying on the brick pavement, unconscious, with a broken left thigh and a severely contused forehead. His chest evidenced signs of internal injuries. The officer sent for a doctor and then began to rub the boy with camphor and brandy, and applied a mustard on his feet and wrists. The child, he observed, "had beautiful black eyes and hair, and was a very handsome boy." The treatment, wrote the officer in a letter a few days after the event, seemed to work: "In a short time he began to breathe better, and opened his eyes, and we all thought he was revived, but it was the last bright gleaming of the wick in the socket before the light is extinguished for ever."

Messengers summoned the president and Varina. When she saw Joseph, she "relieved herself in a flood of tears and wild lamentations." Jefferson kneeled beside his son, squeezed his hands, and watched him die. The Confederate officer, whose name remains unknown to this day, described the president's appearance: "Such a look of petrified, unutterable anguish I never saw. His pale, intellectual face . . . seemed suddenly to burst with unspeakable grief, and thus transfixed into a stony rigidity." Almost thirty years earlier, watching Knox Taylor die had driven him into his "great seclusion." He could not indulge in private grief now. His struggling nation needed him. Davis mastered his emotions in public, but his face could not hide them. "When I recall the picture of our poor president," wrote the officer, "grief-stricken, speechless, tearless and crushed, I can scarcely refrain from tears myself."

That night family and friends and Confederate officials called at the mansion, but Jefferson Davis refused to come downstairs. Above their heads, guests could hear his creaking footsteps on the floorboards as he paced through the night. Mary Chesnut remembered "the tramp of Mr. Davis's step as he walked up and down the room above—not another sound. The whole house [was] as silent as death." The funeral at St. Paul's Church, reported the newspapers, drew the largest crowd of any public event in Richmond since the beginning of the war. Hundreds of children packed the pews, each carrying a green bough or flowers to lay upon Joe's grave. Later, Davis had the porch torn down.

As the Civil War raged on, it was not only Jefferson Davis and Abraham Lincoln who lost those that they loved. In the same year that Willie died, Abraham Lincoln reached out to comfort someone else who had experienced the death of a beloved family member. He wrote a letter to Fanny McCullough, a young girl whose father had been killed in battle. In December 1862, Lincoln received word that Lieutenant Colonel William McCullough, the former clerk of the McLean County Circuit Court in Bloomington, Illinois, had been killed in action on December 5, and that his teenage daughter was overcome with grief. Two days before Christmas, on a day Lincoln might have taken Willie—gone ten months now—to his favorite toy store on New York Avenue, and while Mary worked downstairs with the White House staff making final arrangements for serving Christmas Day dinner to wounded soldiers, the president thought of another child and wrote a condolence letter to Fanny McCullough.

In one of the most moving and revealing letters he ever wrote, Lincoln set down for her his hard-earned knowledge of life and death. It was as if Lincoln had composed the letter not to one sad girl, but to the American people. His words to Fanny might have comforted Jefferson Davis when he grieved over Joseph, or Lincoln's own sons Tad and Robert when they suffered through their father's death.

Washington, December 23, 1862

Dear Fanny

It is with deep regret that I learn of the death of your kind and brave Father; and, especially, that it is affecting your young heart beyond what is common in such cases. In this sad world of ours, sorrow comes to all; and, to the young, it comes with bitterest agony, because it takes them unawares. The older have learned to ever expect it. . . . You can not now realize that you will ever feel better. Is not this so? And yet it is a mistake. You are sure to be happy again. To know this, which is certainly true, will make you some less

miserable now. I have had experience enough to know what I say;
and you need only to believe it, to feel better at once. The memory of
your dear Father, instead of an agony, will yet be a sad sweet feeling
in your heart, of a purer and holier sort than you have known before.
Please present my kind regards to your afflicted mother.

Your sincere friend,
A. Lincoln

On April 17 Jefferson Davis was still on his way to Charlotte. Seventy-two hours after Lincoln's assassination, he still had no idea that Lincoln had been murdered.

On the morning of April 18, the White House gates opened to let the people who had waited all night file into the East Room to see the president's body. Upstairs Mary Lincoln hid in her room with Tad. He would have liked to see the people who came to honor his father. He would, perhaps, have found more comfort in the company of these strangers than alone with his grieving mother.

Jefferson Davis had reached Salisbury, North Carolina. There he read a letter signed by several Confederate officers begging his permission to let their soldiers go home to their families. They wanted to quit the war. Didn't these men know that, like them, Davis worried about his wife and children? But the Confederacy's survival was at stake. If Davis agreed, news of it would spread and infect the whole army. Soon every man would want to leave, and the South would lose. Davis wrote back and refused to give his permission.

As he continued on the road to Charlotte, Jefferson Davis remained cheerful. Burton Harrison described him: "He seemed to have had a great load taken from his mind, to feel relieved of responsibilities, and his conversation was bright and agreeable. He talked of men and of books, particularly of Walter Scott and Byron; of horses and dogs and sports; of the woods and the fields; of trees and many plants; of roads, and how to make them; of the habits of birds, and of a variety of other topics."

The mood in Washington was sad. For the past three days the people had read newspaper stories of the president's assassination and death. Today was their first chance to come face-to-face with his corpse.

Thousands of people walked past the coffin. The viewing of Lincoln's body could have continued all night. But there was work to be done. Thousands more were turned away when it was time to pre-pare the East Room for the funeral. George Harrington had decided that six hundred people needed to attend—but it would be impossible to squeeze six hundred chairs into the East Room. Only a few of the most important guests, including the Lincoln family, would have their own chairs. Carpenters could build risers, or bleachers, for the rest, if they worked through the night.

While men carried stacks of fresh lumber into the East Room and carpenters sawed, hammered, and nailed them, Jefferson Davis spent a quiet night near Concord, North Carolina. Davis expected to enter Charlotte the next day, and he sent a message to his secretary of war telling him to meet with him there.

Even on April 19, the day of Lincoln's funeral, last-minute requests to change the route of the train that would carry his body continued to arrive. One letter, from St. Louis, was addressed to Mary Lincoln. "Please grant to us and the people west of the Mississippi, who loved him so well, the respectful request to direct his body to pass by way of Cincinnati to Saint Louis, thence to Springfield."

But it was too late for Saint Louis and all the other cities that longed for a chance to pay tribute to the president's dead body. Close to midnight on April 19, Edwin Stanton said firmly that there would be no more changes. The route of the train was final. It would start in Washington and travel to Baltimore, Harrisburg, Philadelphia, New York City, Albany, Buffalo, Cleveland, Columbus, Indianapolis, Chicago, and finally to Springfield.

On the morning of the funeral, a reporter was one of the first guests to enter the East Room. He was allowed to approach Lincoln's corpse and invited his readers to do the same: "Approach and look at the dead man. . . . He has not changed one line of his grave, grotesque countenance, nor smoothed out a single feature. . . . The dark eyebrows seem abruptly arched; the beard, which will grow no more, is shaved close, save for the tuft at the short small chin. The mouth is shut, and like that of one who has put the foot down firm, and so are the eyes, which look as calm as slumber. . . . There are sweet roses and early magnolias, and the balmiest of lilies strewn around, as if the flowers had begun to bloom even in his coffin. . . ."

The funeral guests first came to the Treasury Department. From there they crossed a narrow wooden footbridge, built for the occasion, which led into the White House. As they entered the East Room, they were overwhelmed by the decorations, flowers, and the platform where the coffin lay. No president had been so honored in death, not even George Washington.

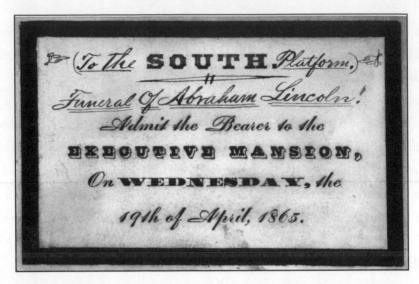

(To the **SOUTH** Platform.)

Funeral Of Abraham Lincoln!

Admit the Bearer to the

EXECUTIVE MANSION,

On **WEDNESDAY**, the

19th of April, 1865.

One of the few surviving invitations to Lincoln's White House funeral.

At exactly ten minutes past noon, a man rose from his chair, approached the coffin, and in a solitary voice broke the hush. The minister spoke the solemn opening words of the Episcopal burial service: "I am the resurrection and the life, saith the Lord; he that believeth in me, though he were dead, yet shall he live; and whosoever liveth and believeth in me shall never die."

A bishop spoke, and then the minister of Lincoln's own church delivered the sermon. Did he remember the day when, in the same White House room a little more than three years ago, he'd given another sermon for Willie Lincoln? "Though our President is slain," he said, "our beloved country is saved; and so we sing of mercy as well as of judgment. Tears of gratitude mingle with those of sorrow, while there is also the dawning of a brighter, happier day upon our stricken and weary land."

While the three ministers spoke for almost two hours, more than a hundred thousand people waited outside the White House. In the driveway, six white horses were harnessed to the magnificent hearse that would carry Lincoln's body. Nearby more than fifty thousand marchers and riders were waiting in line. Another fifty thousand spectators lined Pennsylvania Avenue. Most wore symbols of mourning: black badges containing small photographs of Lincoln, white silk ribbons bordered in black with his picture, small American flags with statements of grief printed in black letters over the stripes, or just simple strips of black crepe wrapped around coat sleeves.

The night before there was not a vacant hotel room in all of Washington, and many people from out of town slept along the streets or in public parks. Some mourners had arrived near the White House as early as sunrise to stake out the best viewing positions. By 10:00 A.M. there were no more places left to stand on Pennsylvania Avenue. Faces filled every window, and children and young men climbed lampposts and trees for a better view. By the time the funeral services ended and the procession to the Capitol got under way, they had already been waiting for hours.

It was a beautiful day. At 2:00 P.M. soldiers in the East Room surrounded the coffin, lifted it from the platform, and carried Abraham Lincoln out of the White House for the last time. They placed the president in the hearse.

Cannon fire announced the start of the procession; guns boomed. Every church and firehouse bell in Washington tolled. Witnesses remembered the sound of the day as much as the sight of it. Tad Lincoln joined the procession, and he and his brother Robert rode in a carriage behind the hearse. The procession was huge. Among the marchers were members of the army, navy, and Marine Corps, and

THE FUNERAL CAR

That conveyed the remains of PRESIDENT LINCOLN from the Executive Mansion to the Capitol, April 19th, 1865.

Entered according to Act of Congress in the year 1865, by CHASE & HAYDN, in the Clerk's Office of the District Court of the United States, for the District of Columbia.

The hearse that carried Lincoln's body down Pennsylvania Avenue.

judges, diplomats, and doctors. One group of marchers suggested the cost of the war: wounded and bandaged veterans, many missing arms or legs, many on crutches.

When the procession reached the other end of Pennsylvania Avenue, soldiers carried the flag-draped coffin up the steps of the Capitol. The crowds watched in silence as the soldiers carried the coffin inside and laid it upon a platform. It was left under the dome with a guard of soldiers keeping watch over the dead president.

CHAPTER NINE

When Jefferson Davis rode into Charlotte, the people there were not happy to see him. Only one man would allow the president of the Confederate States of America to set foot in his home. An officer explained why to Burton Harrison: "The major then took me aside and explained that, though quarters could be found for the rest of us, he had as yet been able to find only one person willing to receive Mr. Davis, saying that people generally were afraid that whoever would entertain him would have his house burned by the enemy."

Not long after his arrival in Charlotte, Davis gave a speech to an audience that included a number of Confederate soldiers:

"My friends, I thank you for this evidence of your affection. If I had come as the bearer of glad tidings, if I had come to announce success at the head of a triumphant army, this is nothing more than I would have expected; but coming as I do, to tell you of a very

great disaster . . . this demonstration of your love fills me with feel-
*ings too deep for **utterance**. This has been a war of the people for*
the people . . . and if they desire to continue the struggle, I am still
ready and willing to devote myself to their cause. True, General
Lee's army has surrendered, but the men are still alive, the cause is
*not yet dead; and only show by your determination and **fortitude***
that you are willing to suffer yet longer, and we may still hope for
success."

At the end of Davis's speech, somebody handed him a telegram
from John C. Breckinridge. Davis read the words in silence: "President
Lincoln was assassinated in the theatre in Washington."

A few minutes later Davis spoke to his secretary of the navy,
Stephen Mallory. In a sad voice, Davis said, "I certainly have no
special regard for Mr. Lincoln; but there are a great many men of
whose end I would much rather have heard than his. I fear it will be
disastrous to our people, and I regret it deeply."

Jefferson Davis tried to understand what Lincoln's murder would
mean for himself and his cause. Who had killed him, and why? What
did this news mean for his retreat, and for his plans to continue the war?
Davis would have found it hard to imagine the strength of emotions
the assassination had stirred up across the country. Had he known, he
might have decided to travel south more quickly.

Despite the disturbing news of Lincoln's death, there were some
people who agreed with Jefferson Davis that it was still possible for the
South to keep the struggle going. On April 19 General Wade Hampton
wrote to his president, encouraging him to continue the fight from
Texas. "Give me a good force of cavalry and I will take them safely

across the Mississippi, and if you desire to go in that direction it will give me great pleasure to escort you. My own mind is made up as to my course. I shall fight as long as my Government remains in existence. . . . If you will allow me to do so, I can bring to your support many strong arms and brave hearts—men who will fight to Texas, and who, if forced from that State, will seek refuge in Mexico rather than in the Union."

In Washington Lincoln's body lay all night in the Capitol. The crowds would have to wait outside. No visitors would be allowed to enter until morning. Thousands of people lined up on East Capitol Street on the afternoon, evening, and night of April 19, waiting for their last chance to see Abraham Lincoln.

The doors to the Capitol were thrown open on the morning of April 20. People passed between two lines of guards on the plaza, entered the building, and split into two lines that passed on either side of the open coffin. The experience lasted only a few moments. Visitors were not allowed to linger, and they walked past the coffin at the rate of more than three thousand an hour. Only the sound of rustling dresses and hoop skirts broke the silence. At 6:00 P.M. the doors were closed and the public viewing ended. If they had been allowed, the people would have kept coming all through the night.

Jefferson Davis awoke in Charlotte on the morning of April 20 still determined to continue the fight. Lincoln's death had changed nothing. Indeed, now that Lincoln's vice president, Andrew Johnson, had become president, Davis believed it was even more important not to give in. Johnson was not as generous a man as Lincoln. If the South surrendered to him, the revenge he would take would be more terrible than any suffered under Abraham Lincoln. Davis had made his decision: The Civil War would go on as long as he lived and as long as his soldiers would fight.

But Davis must have known *this*. Lincoln's murder had placed his life in greater danger. If he was captured by Union troops, they would be tempted to take revenge for Lincoln's murder. Davis might soon join Lincoln in death.

Stanton had chosen the cities the funeral train would stop in. Now he needed to decide who would travel on it. Just a day before the train was to depart Washington, he made his choice of men to take the president home to Springfield. He chose Brigadier General Edward Townsend to command the train and assigned the men who would serve under him.

A Congressman's ticket to ride aboard the Lincoln funeral train.

Stanton also sent Townsend his orders about how everything on the funeral train was to happen. A stickler for detail, he left nothing to chance. At least one officer would be with Lincoln's body at all times. No one who didn't belong on the train should be allowed on. Townsend would report by telegraph the arrival and departure of the train at each city. And the train would have to stick to its timetable. Townsend would be responsible for making sure that, in each city, Lincoln's coffin came back to the funeral train in time for the train to leave on schedule.

Assistant Adjutant General
Edward D. Townsend, commander
of Lincoln's funeral train.

Stanton issued another order on April 20. It was a public announcement offering a hundred thousand dollar reward for the capture of Abraham Lincoln's assassin, John Wilkes Booth, and for his coconspirators John Surratt and George Atzerodt. Six days after the assassination, the murderer was still at large. Both the fleeing Confederate president and the killer of the Union president were still on the run. To anyone who dared to help Booth during his escape from justice, Stanton promised the punishment of death.

On the same day that Stanton announced the reward, Jefferson Davis wondered if Lincoln's murder might help his cause. "It is difficult to judge of the effect" of the murder, he wrote. "His successor [Andrew Johnson] is a worse man, but has less influence. . . . [I] am not without hope that recent disaster may awake the **dormant** energy and develop the patriotism which sustained us in the first years of the War."

Davis was struggling unsuccessfully to make sure that his

remaining soldiers had what they needed to fight. "General Duke's brigade is here without saddles," he wrote on April 20. "There are none here or this side of Augusta. Send on to this point 600, or as many as can be had." In another letter Davis asked for cannons and more men. Travel was becoming increasingly difficult. On the evening of April 20, John C. Breckinridge, Davis's secretary of war, wrote from Salisbury, North Carolina, to Davis in Charlotte: "We have had great difficulty in reaching this place. The train from Charlotte which was to have met me here has not arrived." President Davis replied promptly: "Train will start for you at midnight with guard."

On April 20 Robert E. Lee was at home in Richmond. He had no army to command. He knew that President Davis was still trying to continue to fight the war. Lee thought he was wrong to do so. Any further fighting must, he believed, turn into bloody, lawless, **guerrilla warfare**. Better an honorable surrender than that. Lee wrote a remarkable letter to his commander in chief. He urged Jefferson Davis to surrender: "From what I have seen and learned, I believe an army cannot be organized or supported in Virginia, and as far as I know the condition of affairs, the country east of the Mississippi is morally and physically unable to maintain the contest. . . . A partisan war may be continued . . . causing individual suffering and devastation of the country, but I see no prospect by that means of achieving a separate independence. It is for Your Excellency to decide, should you agree with me in opinion, what is proper to be done. . . . I would recommend measures be taken for . . . the restoration of peace."

Davis never got Lee's letter. But even if he had, it would not have convinced him to surrender. Davis still had faith that by crossing to the west of the Mississippi, he would be able to continue the war. Indeed, the arrival in Charlotte that very day of several cavalry units gave Davis new hope.

Davis had almost decided to leave the country, but when these soldiers and their horses arrived in Charlotte, he changed his mind. "Troops began to come into Charlotte, however . . . and there was much talk among them of crossing the Mississippi and continuing the war," remembered Stephen Mallory. "They seemed determined to get across the river and fight it out, and whenever they encountered Mr. Davis they cheered and sought to encourage him. . . . He became indifferent to his own safety, thinking only of gathering together a body of troops to make head against the foe and so arouse the people to arms."

At 6:00 A.M. on Friday, April 21, one week after the assassination, an escort arrived at the Capitol to accompany Lincoln's body to the funeral train. Soldiers removed the coffin from the platform, carried it down the stairs, and placed it in a horse-drawn hearse. It was not supposed to be a grand or official procession. There were no drummers, no bands, and no train of marchers. It was just a short trip from the east front plaza of the Capitol to the Baltimore and Ohio Railroad station.

But that did not stop the crowds. Several thousand onlookers lined the route and surrounded the station entrance. Edwin Stanton supervised the procession himself to make sure that the transfer of Abraham Lincoln's body from the Capitol to the funeral train was done with simplicity, dignity, and honor.

Earlier that morning another hearse had arrived at the station. It had come from Oak Hill Cemetery in Georgetown. When the soldiers

Mourning ribbon worn by members of the
United States Military Rail Road.

carried Abraham Lincoln aboard his private railroad car at 7:30 A.M., the body of his dead son Willie was already there, waiting for him. Once Lincoln had planned to collect the boy himself and take his coffin home. Now two coffins shared the presidential car.

Members of the honor guard took their places beside the coffin. The train would not take aboard the hearse and horses which had carried Lincoln's body to the railroad station. Instead, in every city where the train would stop for funeral services, local officials would provide a horse-drawn hearse to take the coffin from the train.

At 7:50 A.M. Robert Lincoln boarded the train. He would not ride all the way to Illinois. He planned to ride the train part of the way, then return to Washington to wrap up his father's affairs. Mary Lincoln did not board the train; nor did she appear at the station to see her husband off. And she did not allow Tad to go.

Tad should have gone to the station and then ridden with his father all the way back to Illinois. After Willie's death, Tad and his father were always together. Sometimes Tad fell asleep in the president's office, and Lincoln would lift the boy over his shoulder and carry him off to bed. Tad loved to go on trips with his father. He loved to see soldiers, and he enjoyed wearing—and posing for photos—in a child-size Union army officer's uniform, complete with a tiny sword, that Lincoln had given him. Tad would have marveled at the sights and sounds along the sixteen-hundred-mile journey. And he would have been proud of, and taken comfort from, the honor paid to his father. But, kept in the White House, Tad saw none of this.

Two more men boarded the train as it waited at the station. In the days to come, the success or failure of this mission would depend upon their work. They were the "body men," embalmer Dr. Brown and undertaker Frank Sands. For the next thirteen days, it would be their job to keep Abraham Lincoln's corpse looking as lifelike as possible.

At exactly 8:00 A.M. the wheels of the engine turned, and the eight railroad cars it pulled began to move.

Lincoln's train would reach Baltimore in four hours. No one knew exactly what would happen at the first stop outside Washington. No one anticipated what was to come: bonfires, torches, arches of flowers, hand-painted signs, banners, and masses of people along the way at all hours of the day or night. Parents held out sleepy-eyed infants and even uncomprehending babes in arms, so that one day they could tell their children: "*You* were there. You saw Father Abraham pass by."

Without anyone in the government ordering it, this train became more than the funeral for one dead man. Somewhere between

Washington and Springfield, the train became a symbol of the cost of the Civil War. It represented a mournful homecoming for all the men—Union and Confederate—who had died on the battlefield. It was as if an army of the dead—and not one solitary man—rode aboard that train.

Lincoln's funeral car.

CHAPTER TEN

But this transformation had not yet taken place as the train approached Baltimore. The whole state of Maryland, and Baltimore in particular, were known for being unfriendly to Lincoln. Four years ago, on his way to become president, Lincoln's train had traveled through Baltimore. People there were rumored to be plotting to kill him. Lincoln passed through the city in secrecy in the middle of the night.

But now all was peaceful as the train arrived at Baltimore at 10:00 A.M. Townsend telegraphed Stanton promptly: "Just arrived all safe." Thousands of sincere mourners stood in heavy rain to await the president. The honor guard aboard the train carried the coffin from the car and placed it in a hearse drawn by four black horses.

The hearse was designed to display the coffin. According to one spectator, "The body of this hearse was almost entirely composed of plate glass, which enabled the vast crowd . . . to have a full view of the coffin. The supports of the top were draped with black cloth and white silk, and the top of the car was handsomely decorated with black plumes."

A procession got under way and marched to the Merchant's Exchange. It took three hours to reach Calvert Street. The column halted, the hearse drove to the southern entrance of the Exchange, and Lincoln's bearers carried him inside. There they laid the coffin beneath a dome, upon a platform about three feet tall, with columns on the four corners. A canopy fourteen feet tall was draped with black cloth, trimmed with silver fringe, and decorated with silver stars. Around the platform, Townsend saw, "were tastefully arranged evergreens, wreaths, calla-lilies, and other **choice** flowers."

In Baltimore there would be no ceremonies, sermons, or speeches; there was no time for that. Instead, as soon as Lincoln was in position, guards threw the doors open and the public mourners filed in. Over the next four hours, thousands viewed the body. The upper part of the coffin was open to reveal Lincoln's face and chest.

In Baltimore, Edward Townsend established two rules. First, no one except the officers and men of the United States army traveling aboard the train was ever allowed to touch the president's coffin. Townsend was firm: "No bearers, except the veteran guard, were ever suffered to handle the President's coffin." Second, Townsend had forbidden mourners to get too close to the open coffin, to touch the president's body, to kiss him, or to place anything, including flowers, in the coffin. Any person who violated these rules would be seized at once and removed from Lincoln's presence.

At about 2:30 P.M., with thousands of citizens, black and white, still waiting in line to see the president, local officials ended the viewing. Lincoln's bearers closed the coffin and carried it back to the hearse.

A second procession delivered Lincoln's body to the North Central Railway station in time for the scheduled 3:00 P.M. departure for Harrisburg, Pennsylvania.

The first stop had gone well. General Townsend sent a telegram to the Secretary of War:

BALTIMORE, April 21, 1865.

Hon. E. M. STANTON,
Secretary of War:
Ceremonies very imposing. Dense crowd lined the streets; chiefly laboring classes, white and black. Perfect order throughout. Many men and women in tears. Arrangements admirable. Start for Harrisburg [Pennsylvania] at 3 p.m.

E. D. TOWNSEND,
Assistant Adjutant-General

On the way to Harrisburg, the train stopped briefly at York, where the women of the city had asked permission to lay a wreath of flowers upon Lincoln's coffin. Edward Townsend allowed six women to come aboard. While a band played a **dirge** and bells tolled, they approached the funeral car, stepped inside, and laid their large wreath of red and white flowers on the coffin. The women wept bitterly as they left the train. Soon, at the next stop, their flowers would be pushed aside in favor of others.

The train arrived at Harrisburg, capital of Pennsylvania, at 8:20 P.M. on Friday, April 21. Townsend reported to Edwin Stanton: "Arrived here safely. Everything goes on well." It was dark and a heavy rain was falling. "Slowly through the muddy streets, followed by two of the guard of honor and the faithful sergeants, the hearse wended its way to the Capitol," Townsend wrote.

Even in the rain, thousands of onlookers followed the hearse to the State House. To the boom of cannon firing once a minute, the coffin was carried inside and laid on a platform. Lincoln was on view until midnight, and again at 7:00 A.M. the next morning, Saturday, April 22. The coffin was closed at 9:00 A.M. At 10:00 A.M., as a band played, drums beat, and soldiers marched or rode their horses, a hearse carried Lincoln back to the train.

On April 22, while Abraham Lincoln was on the move, Jefferson Davis had still not left Charlotte, North Carolina. Lincoln's murder had placed Davis in greater peril, but the Confederate president didn't rush to escape. Davis acted as a man making a careful retreat, not fleeing for his life.

Davis was not the only one who wanted to keep fighting. General Wade Hampton wrote to him again on April 22, encouraging him to make a run for Texas. "If you should propose to cross the Mississippi River I can bring many good men to escort you over," he told Davis. "My men are in hand and ready to follow me anywhere . . . I write hurriedly, as the messenger is about to leave. If I can serve you or my country by any further fighting you have only to tell me so. My plan is to collect all the men who will stick to their colors, and to get to Texas."

Lincoln's funeral train left Harrisburg forty-five minutes early. At every station, and along the railroad tracks between them, people gathered to watch the train pass by. For miles before Philadelphia, unbroken lines of people stood and watched along both sides of the tracks.

The train arrived in Philadelphia before 5:00 P.M. on Saturday, April 22. As soon as the engine rolled into the station, a single cannon shot announced to the city that Lincoln had arrived. Townsend sent off a telegram to Stanton: "We have arrived here safely. Everything is in good order." The crowd was immense.

At 5:15 P.M. the hearse, drawn by eight black horses, got under way. The huge procession took almost three hours to reach Independence Hall. The square in front of the hall shone with red, white, and blue lights. As guns fired and bells tolled, Abraham Lincoln's body was carried into the building where the Declaration of Independence and the Constitution had been debated. He was laid at the foot of the Liberty Bell.

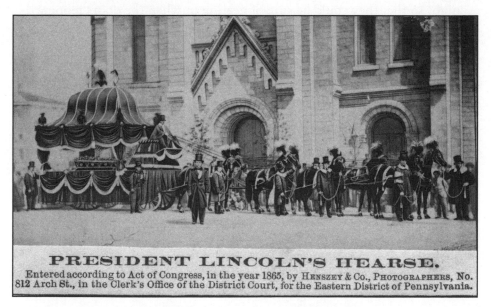

PRESIDENT LINCOLN'S HEARSE.
Entered according to Act of Congress, in the year 1865, by HENSZEY & Co., PHOTOGRAPHERS, No. 812 Arch St., in the Clerk's Office of the District Court, for the Eastern District of Pennsylvania.

President Lincoln's hearse in Philadelphia.

The inside of Independence Hall was draped with black cloth. It hung everywhere: from the walls, from the chandelier over the coffin, and from most of the paintings. A white marble statue of George Washington remained uncovered, and it stood out like a ghost in the blackened room.

Candles burned among twenty-five vases of rare flowers. "A delicious perfume stole through every part of the Hall," one observer wrote. But no one mentioned the practical purpose the sweet-smelling flowers served. Abraham Lincoln had been dead a week. Fragrant flowers would hide the odor of his slowly decaying flesh.

At midnight the public came in. They entered by temporary stairs that had been made through two windows and exited through a second set of stairs through two more windows. The coffin was closed at 2:00 A.M. on Sunday, April 23, and would be reopened at 6:00 A.M. Many people in line stood outside Independence Hall the rest of the night so that they could be sure of getting in when the doors reopened in several hours. After the long wait, mourners were given only a few seconds to view Lincoln.

The vast crowds had become dangerous, and the newspaper reported accidents. "Hundreds of persons were seriously injured from being pressed in the mob," one story read, "and many fainting females were **extricated** by the police and military and conveyed to places of security. Many women lost their bonnets, while others had nearly every article of clothing torn from their persons."

On Sunday, April 23, while the crowds of Philadelphia filed past Lincoln's coffin, Jefferson Davis went to church in Charlotte. The minister gave an angry sermon criticizing Lincoln's murder that seemed aimed at the Confederate president. "As Mr. Davis walked away," Burton Harrison remembered, "he said, with a smile, 'I think the preacher directed his remarks at me; and he really seems to fancy that I had something to do with the assassination.'"

The same day the president wrote to Varina. It was a long, thoughtful letter. Less hopeful, more realistic, but not beaten yet, Davis apologized to his beloved companion for taking her on the lifelong journey that had led to this fate. If Lee had not surrendered, he told her, or if his soldiers had been willing to come back to the fight, all might still have been well. "Had that army held together I am now confident we could have successfully executed the plan which I sketched to you and would have been to-day on the high road to independence." Now he was struggling to decide what was best to do.

"I have sacrificed so much for the cause of the Confederacy that I can measure my ability to make any further sacrifice required, and am assured there is but one to which I am not equal, my Wife and my Children. . . . for myself it may be that our Enemy will prefer to banish me, it may be that a devoted band of Cavalry will cling to me and that I can force my way across the Missi. [Mississippi] and if nothing can be done there which it will be proper to do, then I can go to Mexico and have the world from which to choose. . . . Dear Wife this is not the fate to which I invited [you] when the future was rose-colored to us both; but I know you will bear it even better than myself and that of us two I alone will ever look back reproachfully on my past career. . . . Farewell my Dear; there may be better things

in store for us than are now in view, but my love is all I have
to offer and that has the value of a thing long possessed and sure
not to be lost."

In Philadelphia, Abraham Lincoln's funeral procession left Independence Hall at 1:00 A.M. on Monday, April 24. Despite the late hour thousands of citizens from every part of the city joined the march. It took three hours, until almost 4:00 A.M., to reach Kensington Station. Townsend kept Stanton informed: "We start for New York at 4 o'clock [A.M.]. No accident so far. Nothing can exceed the demonstration of affection for Mr. Lincoln. Arrangements most perfect." The funeral train departed a few minutes later, headed for New York City.

Thousands of people lined the tracks on the journey. The train reached Jersey City, New Jersey, at 9:00 A.M. on Monday, April 24. There the presidential car was set loose from the train and rolled onto a ferryboat. At 10:00 A.M. Lincoln's ferry landed in Manhattan and the procession to City Hall began.

In New York Lincoln's hearse was fourteen feet long and fifteen feet wide, drawn by sixteen gray horses. Draped in black cloth with silver fringe, it had an empty "temple of liberty" on top to symbolize the nation without the president to lead it. Above the temple was a large golden eagle with outstretched wings.

City Hall had been transformed beyond recognition. Everything was draped in black cloth. Even the windows were covered with black curtains, so that the light was dim and somber. A square platform had been prepared for the coffin; an arch rose over it, with another eagle perched above a bust of Lincoln himself.

The extravagant New York City funeral hearse.
On the right, City Hall is draped in mourning.

In ceremonies at Union Square, the famous speaker George Bancroft gave a long speech. "The President of the United States has fallen by the hands of an assassin," he declared. "The wailings of the millions attend his remains as they are borne on solemn procession over our great rivers, along the seaside, beyond the mountains, across the prairie, to their final resting place. . . . Happy was his life, for he was the restorer of the Republic; he was happy in his death, for the manner of his end will plead forever for the union of the States and the freedom of man."

New York had outdone all other cities on the funeral route so far. To anyone in the streets of Manhattan on April 24, 1865, it didn't seem possible that any other city along the route could do anything more magnificent to honor Lincoln than what New York had done.

The coffin was closed at 11:00 A.M. on Tuesday, April 25. At 12:30 P.M. the hearse, this time drawn by sixteen white horses, took Lincoln to the station of the Hudson River Railroad. One hundred twenty-five thousand people had viewed the corpse. Five hundred thousand stood along the procession route. "A time for weeping, But vengeance is not sleeping" read one of the signs that the hearse passed by.

The memorial arch above the tracks at Sing-Sing, New York.

At 3:00 P.M. the head of the procession arrived at the railroad station. It took another half hour for Lincoln's hearse to arrive. General Townsend telegraphed the secretary of war:

NEW YORK CITY, April 25, 1865

Hon. E. M. STANTON:
The ceremonies and procession have been most complete and imposing. Everything passed off admirably. I have examined the remains and they are in perfect preservation. We start for Albany at 4.15 p.m.

E. D. TOWNSEND,
Assistant Adjutant-General.

The engine steamed north along the Hudson River. General Townsend was surprised at how many people he saw when he looked out the window. "The line of the Hudson River road seemed alive with people," he remembered. At 6:20 P.M., the train stopped across the river from the United States Military Academy at West Point. The corps of cadets assembled to honor their fallen commander in chief. They passed through the funeral car and saluted. Then the train moved on.

After darkness fell, the train passed through the town of Hudson. The people there had prepared a scene, almost a little play. There was a coffin on a platform, with a woman dressed in white mourning over it, and a soldier and a sailor standing at either end. "While a band of young women dressed in white sang a dirge," Townsend wrote later, "two others in black entered the funeral-car." The women laid an arrangement of flowers on Lincoln's coffin. Then they "knelt for a moment of silence, and quietly withdrew."

At 1:30 A.M. on April 26, Lincoln's coffin was placed in the assembly chamber of the State Capitol in Albany and the viewing began. It was the middle of the night, but seventy mourners per minute came to see Lincoln's corpse, more than four thousand an hour.

But something else happened at Albany—a telegram from Edwin Stanton caught up with Edward Townsend. While the funeral train had been in New York City, a photograph had been taken of Lincoln's corpse. This was the first picture that had been taken of Lincoln since he had died. Stanton had learned of it by reading the newspapers. He sent off a furious message.

WAR DEPARTMENT,
Washington City, April 25, 1865—11.40 p.m.

Brigadier-General TOWNSEND,
Adjutant General, New York:
I see by the New York papers this evening that a photograph of the corpse of President Lincoln was allowed taken yesterday at New York. I cannot sufficiently express my surprise and disapproval of such an act while the body was in your charge. You will report what officers of the funeral escort were or ought to have been on duty at the time this was done, and immediately relieve them and order them to Washington. You will also direct the provost-marshal to go to the photographer, seize and destroy the plates and any pictures and engravings that may have been made, and consider yourself responsible if the offense is repeated.
EDWIN M. STANTON,
Secretary of War

Stanton probably assumed that close-up images had been made of Lincoln's face. By the time Lincoln was photographed in New York, he had been dead for nine days. There was only so much the undertakers could do. Stanton no doubt feared that pictures of Lincoln's face in a state of gruesome decay would be distributed to anyone who wanted to buy them.

Townsend received the telegram in Albany, New York. He knew his boss well, including his temper. Once Stanton learned the full story, Townsend feared, he would be completely enraged—because it was Townsend, and no one else, who had allowed Lincoln's corpse to be photographed. In fact, Townsend had posed in the picture, standing beside the coffin.

Townsend decided, before others could report what he had done, to confess.

He sent a telegram to Stanton. "The photograph was taken while I was present," he wrote. "I regret your disapproval, but it did not strike me as objectionable under the circumstances as it was done." He would transmit the order about destroying the plates and the photographs. Who, he asked, should be in charge of the funeral train if he obeyed Stanton's orders and returned the person responsible—himself—to Washington?

When Stanton learned that it was Townsend who had allowed the photographs to be made, he decided not to take away his command. The train was on the move, and there was nobody else available to take charge. But Stanton was still not happy. "The taking of photographs was expressly forbidden by Mrs. Lincoln," he told Townsend. He worried "that her feelings and the feelings of her family will be greatly wounded."

"I was not aware of Mrs. Lincoln's wishes," Townsend responded, "or the picture would not have been taken." He added, "It seemed to me the picture would be gratifying, a grand view of what thousands saw and thousands could not see."

Later Townsend sent yet another telegram, describing the photograph. It was not, as Stanton probably feared, a close-up view of Lincoln's face, but a picture of the coffin, draped in black and surrounded by flags, as it had been viewed by thousands of New Yorkers. "The effect of the picture would be general," Townsend assured Stanton, "taking in the whole scene, but not giving the features of the corpse."

Stanton did not punish Townsend for what he had done. But he did order the photographs and the glass plate negatives seized. To this day no one knows what became of them. Perhaps Stanton destroyed the prints and smashed the glass negatives. Perhaps he stored them somewhere no one has ever found them.

But Stanton could not resist saving for himself at least one image of Lincoln's corpse. Almost a century after Lincoln's death, a sole surviving photograph made from one of the negatives was discovered, stored with Stanton's personal files. Perhaps Stanton saved it for history. Or perhaps he intended that it should never be seen, and that it remain for his eyes only, a vivid reminder of the death of Abraham Lincoln.

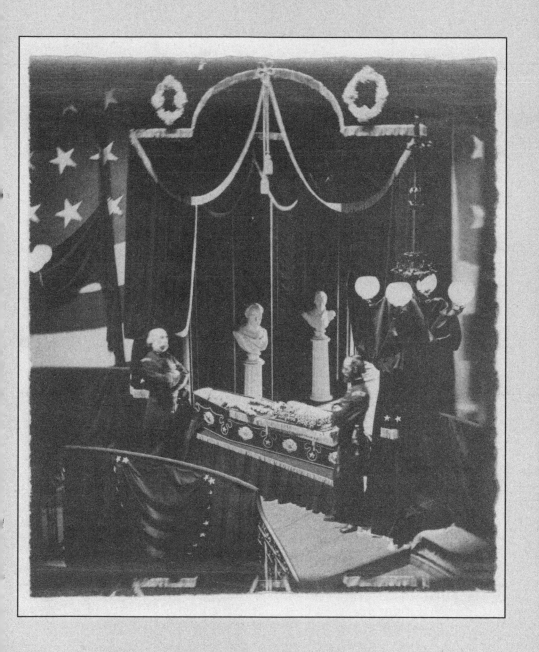

The notorious Gurney image, taken inside New York City Hall. Edward D. Townsend stands at the foot of the coffin in the only surviving photograph of Lincoln in death.

CHAPTER ELEVEN

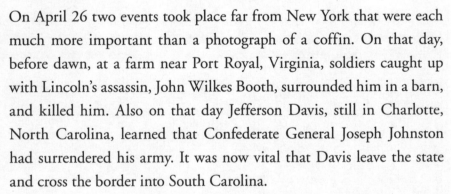

On April 26 two events took place far from New York that were each much more important than a photograph of a coffin. On that day, before dawn, at a farm near Port Royal, Virginia, soldiers caught up with Lincoln's assassin, John Wilkes Booth, surrounded him in a barn, and killed him. Also on that day Jefferson Davis, still in Charlotte, North Carolina, learned that Confederate General Joseph Johnston had surrendered his army. It was now vital that Davis leave the state and cross the border into South Carolina.

Before Jefferson Davis left Charlotte, he wrote to General Wade Hampton: "If you think it better you can, with the approval of General Johnston, select now . . . the small body of men and join me at once."

Then, in haste, Davis wrote a letter to Varina. "The Cavalry is now the last hope," he told her. "I will organize what force of Cavalry can be had. [General] Hampton offers to lead them, and thinks he can force his way across the Mississippi. The route will be too rough and perilous for you and children to go with me. . . . Will try to see you soon."

The funeral train left Albany at 4:00 P.M., Wednesday, April 26. Mile by mile, the crowds got thicker wherever the train was scheduled to pass. At Schenectady railroad signalmen waved small flags bordered with black. The train stopped briefly in Little Falls, where a band played a dirge while women presented flowers for the coffin.

At 11:15 P.M., the train made a short stop at Syracuse, where soldiers paid honors, a choir sang hymns, and a little girl handed a small bouquet to a congressman on the train. A note attached to the flowers read: "The last tribute from Mary Virginia Raynor, a little girl of three years of age."

The train arrived in Rochester at 3:20 A.M. on April 27, and the former president of the United States, Millard Fillmore, got on board for the next stop, Buffalo. Three and a half hours later, tolling bells and booming cannons awoke the citizens of Buffalo who had not already assembled at the railroad station. Abraham Lincoln had arrived.

At 8:00 A.M. a procession, which included President Fillmore, went with the hearse to St. James Hall. Under a simple canopy of drooping black crepe, they laid the coffin on a platform while a musical group sang "Rest, Spirit, Rest." Women from the Unitarian church placed an anchor of white camellias at the foot of the coffin. For more than ten hours, thousands of people, including many Canadians who had crossed the border for the occasion, viewed Lincoln's body. It was during that day that Townsend and the others in Buffalo learned that John Wilkes Booth had been captured and killed.

★ ★ ★

As Lincoln's train pulled out of Buffalo, Jefferson Davis spent the night at Yorkville, South Carolina. He was taking his time. His journey south was more like a farewell procession than a speedy flight.

On the night of April 27, General Wade Hampton wanted to lead his cavalry to the president's side. But he was worried about what to do. His commander, General Johnston, had surrendered. This meant that Hampton was supposed to surrender, too. But he had already promised to come to Jefferson Davis's aid. Whatever he did, he would risk dishonor. Hampton wrote a letter to General Johnston: "By your advice I went to consult with President Davis. . . . A plan was agreed on to enable him to leave the country. . . . On my return here I find myself not only powerless to assist him, but placed myself in a position of great delicacy. . . . If I do not accompany him I shall never cease to reproach myself, and if I go with him I may go under the ban of outlawry. I choose the latter, because I believe it to be my duty to do so. . . . I shall not ask a man to go with me. Should any join me, they will . . . like myself, [be] willing to sacrifice everything for the cause. . . ."

Other cavalry units also hoped to ride to Davis's side, not to protect him, but to kill or capture him. Now that the manhunt for Booth had ended, Stanton could focus on Jefferson Davis. On Wednesday, April 27, one day after the actor was shot and killed, Stanton telegraphed an order to do whatever was necessary to capture the Confederate president and the gold he was rumored to be carrying. "[S]pare no exertion to stop Davis and his plunder. Push the enemy as hard as you can in every direction," Stanton ordered.

Meanwhile, the funeral train rode on in the darkness of the night through New York State. "The night journey of the 27th and 28th was all through torches, bonfires, mourning drapery, **mottoes**, and solemn music," Townsend remembered. At 12:10 A.M., Friday, April 28, the train passed through Dunkirk on the shore of Lake Erie. There, thirty-six young women, one for each state of the Union, appeared on the railway platform. Each was dressed in white, with a broad black scarf resting across one shoulder and holding in her right hand a national flag.

The train stopped at 1:00 A.M. in Westfield. In 1861, when Lincoln had been on his way to Washington, he had stopped here to speak to Grace Bedell, a little girl who had written him a letter encouraging him to grow a beard. Now, four years later, a delegation of five women led by Grace's mother, whose husband had been killed in the war, came aboard the train with a wreath of flowers and a cross. Sobbing, they approached Lincoln's coffin and were allowed, as a special privilege, to touch and kiss it.

The train crossed the Pennsylvania state line and continued into Ohio.

On April 28 Davis and his entourage stopped at Broad River, South Carolina, to rest and eat lunch. They began talking of how the war had destroyed all that they owned. Most of their homes and property had been burned or taken by the Union armies.

Jefferson Davis was no exception. Two years ago, in 1863, an officer had brought word to Davis that his beloved plantation, Brier Field, would soon fall into the hands of Union soldiers. Friends urged Davis to order Confederate soldiers to rush to his plantation to rescue his slaves and other property and move them somewhere safe. Although he hated to lose Brier Field, Davis was outraged at the suggestion. "The President of the Confederacy cannot employ men to take care of his property," he said. Later, when Union forces threatened his other house in Jackson, Mississippi, Davis again refused to send soldiers to protect his home.

On April 28 Varina Davis, then in Abbeville, replied to her husband's most recent letter. He had accused himself of bringing her to ruin. She reminded him that she had never expected a life of privilege and ease. "You must remember that you did not invite me to a great Hero's home, but to that of a plain farmer," she told him. "I know there is a future for you." But not, she thought, in South Carolina, Georgia, or Florida. Varina advised him to give up the cause east of the Mississippi River. "I have seen a great many men who have gone through [Abbeville]—not one has talked fight—A Stand cannot be made in this country." She advised him to try to relocate the fighting west of the Mississippi.

Continuing on the road, Jefferson Davis gave away his last gold coin. John Reagan, the Confederate postmaster general, watched him do it. "On our way to Abbeville, South Carolina, President Davis and I . . . passed a cabin on the roadside, where a lady was standing in the door. He turned aside and requested a drink of water, which she brought. While he was drinking, a little baby hardly old enough to walk crawled down the steps. The lady asked whether this was not president Davis." On hearing that he was, "she pointed to the little boy and said, 'He is named for you.' Mr. Davis took a gold coin from his pocket and asked her to keep it for his namesake. It was a foreign piece, and from its size I supposed it to be worth three or four dollars. As we rode off he told me that it was the last coin he had. . . ."

The president of the Confederacy was now penniless. Yes, he was traveling with half a million dollars in gold and silver, but that money belonged to the Confederate government, not its president. Davis would not use it for himself.

Now the only riches he possessed were the love and goodwill of the people. He hoped that, in the days ahead, as he pushed deeper into the South, the people there would show him better hospitality than he had received in Greensboro and Charlotte, North Carolina. His aides assured him that it would be so. In South Carolina and Georgia, they promised, the people still loved him and believed in the cause of the South.

Lincoln's train arrived at Cleveland on the morning of Friday, April 28. Thirty-six cannons fired a salute. There was not one public building or hall in all of Cleveland big enough to hold all the people who would want to view the president's body, so the citizens built an outdoor pavilion. They could make it look like a Chinese pagoda. No one would forget *that*.

The hearse took Lincoln's coffin to the public square where the pagoda had been erected. The wooden structure, fourteen feet high, was covered with canvas, silk, cloth roses, golden eagles, and "immense plumes of black crepe." Inside it was full of flowers. Evergreens covered the walls, and thick matting carpeted the floor to muffle the sound of footsteps. Over the roof, stretched between two flagpoles, was a streamer that read, in Latin, "Dead, he will be loved the same."

The embalmer opened the coffin to check on the body. Lincoln's face was turning darker by the day, which the embalmers tried to conceal by coating the skin with chalk-white potions.

All through the day and night, in a steady rain, the people came, one hundred thousand of them. The coffin was closed at 10:10 P.M. and was carried to the hearse. Just then the rain turned into a downpour. The storm lasted for most of the night as the train steamed through Ohio from Cleveland to the state capital, Columbus.

In Cleveland, crowds wait to view Lincoln's corpse in the celebrated "pagoda" pavilion.

The foul weather did not stop the people from turning out along the tracks. Bonfires and torches burned. Buildings were draped in black cloth. Bells tolled and flags were lowered to half-staff. Five miles from Columbus, the passengers on the train noticed a heart-felt tribute that stood out among all the official processions and ceremonies.

They saw "an aged woman bare headed . . . tears coming down her furrowed cheeks, holding in her right hand a sable scarf and in her left a bouquet of wild flowers, which she stretched imploringly toward the funeral car." Her gesture was simple and touching. Abraham Lincoln would have noticed her. She might have reminded him of his stepmother, who had been waiting long years for him to return. "I knowed when he went away he'd never come back alive," she had said when she'd heard of his murder.

The train pulled into Columbus at 7:30 A.M., Saturday, April 29.

Again there was a procession and a viewing in yet another building draped with black and overflowing with flowers. The hearse
drove off and, as usual, left behind on the train a coffin that had
accompanied Lincoln from Washington. In newspaper stories of the
funeral train, little mention was made of Willie Lincoln. His small
coffin was never unloaded from the train. But in Columbus Willie
Lincoln was not forgotten. General Townsend recalled: "While at
Columbus I received a note from a lady," he wrote, "accompanying a
little cross made of wild violets. The note said that the writer's little
girls had gone to the woods in the early morning and gathered the
flowers with which [they] had wrought the cross. They desired it
might be laid on little Willie's coffin, 'they felt so sorry for him.'"

On April 29 Jefferson Davis crossed the Saluda River in South
Carolina. Federal soldiers were having a difficult time picking up his
trail. One Yankee cavalryman complained, "The white people seemed
to be doing all they could to throw us off Davis' trail and impart false
information to their slaves, knowing the latter would lose no time in
bringing it to us."

The Union general in charge of the manhunt for Davis did not
know exactly where to look—but it didn't really matter. He expected
Davis to head for Georgia, or perhaps make it all the way to Florida,
and so he planned to blanket the entire region with troops. If Davis
went south, someone would find him.

At 8:00 P.M. tolling bells signaled the train's departure from
Columbus. It steamed west and crossed into Indiana in the middle
of the night. At 7:00 A.M. on Sunday, April 30, the train arrived in
Indianapolis. In the rain, a hearse fourteen feet high and fourteen

TERRE HAUTE & RICHMOND RAILROAD.

FUNERAL CEREMONIES

OF THE LATE

PRESIDENT LINCOLN!

To be Observed at Indianapolis Sunday, April 30, 1865.

SPECIAL TRAINS will be run at Half the regular Fare on the above date, according to the following schedule, to carry all persons wishing to participate in the above ceremonies.

GOING EAST.				GOING WEST.		
No. 3	Leave.	No. 1.		No. 2.	Arrive	No. 4.
6.30	A.M.		Terre Haute,	7.20	P.M.	
6.48	"		Wood's Mill,	7.02	"	
7.00	"		Staunton,	6.50	"	
7.15	"		Brazil,	6.38	"	
7.25	"		Harmony,	6.27	"	
7.41	"		Reelsville,	6.10	"	
8.02	"		Junction,	5.52	"	
8.15	"	7.30	A.M. Greencastle,	5.45	"	6.20	P.M.
8.30	"	7.46	" Fillmore,	5.23	"	6.05	"
8.41	"	7.57	" Coatsville,	5.12	"	5.53	"
8.49	"	8.05	" Amo,	5.05	"	5.45	"
9.01	"	8.18	" Clayton,	4.52	"	5.32	"
9.11	"	8.30	" Cartersburg,	4.41	"	5.18	"
9.20	"	8.40	" Plainfield,	4.33	"	5.08	"
			Summit,				"
9.30	"	8.52	" Bridgeport,	4.22	"	4.53	"
9.50	A.M.	9.15	A.M. Indianapolis,	4.00	P.M.	4.30	P.M.
	Arrive.				Leave.		

Tickets will be on sale at all the principal Stations, for one Full Fare to Indianapolis and return. Passengers must purchase Tickets before taking the Trains, or Full Fare will be collected.

Passengers are specially requested to purchase their Tickets, as much as possible, on Saturday, the 29th inst.

Tickets of Passengers from the Evansville and Albany Roads will be taken on the Evening Express of the 29th inst., and will be good to return on the morning Mail Train of Monday, May 1st; all other Tickets will not be good except on the Sunday Trains.

Trains Nos. 2 and 3 will make all the usual stops, on signal, West, but none East of Greencastle.

Nos. 1 and 4 will make all the usual stops, on signal, East of Greencastle.

CHAS. WOOD, Sec'y.   **R. E. RICKER, Sup't.**

INDIANAPOLIS, APRIL 26TH, 1865.

Railroads ran special trains to the cities where Lincoln's body lay in state.

feet long drew the president to the dome of the state capitol, where he would lie in state for more than fifteen hours and be seen by more than a hundred thousand people.

At midnight the train set off again for Chicago.

Around the same time, Varina wrote a letter to her husband. "I have given up hope of seeing you but it is not for long," she told him. She hoped to "take a ship or what else I can . . . still think we will make out somehow. May the Lord have you in his holy keeping I constantly, and earnestly pray. . . . The children have been more than good, and talk much of you. . . ."

The funeral train reached Chicago on May 1 at 11:00 A.M. Guns fired to announce its arrival. Tens of thousands of people had been waiting in the streets for hours. One spectator wrote that "every window was filled with faces, and every door-step . . . filled with human beings." A newspaper even suggested that the rough waters of Lake Michigan "suddenly calmed from their angry roar into solemn silence" as if they, too, mourned for Lincoln.

At the train station a huge funeral arch had been set up. Lincoln's coffin was laid near it, and thirty-six high school girls, each dressed in white and wearing a black sash, placed a flower on the coffin. Then the honor guard placed the coffin in the hearse, and the procession to the courthouse began. Ten thousand children marched in line behind groups of soldiers and city officials. More than 120,000 people took part in or witnessed the procession. One of them, Daniel Brooks, had, as a sixteen-year-old boy, taken part in George Washington's funeral procession in 1799.

The Chicago funeral arch.

The hearse stopped at the courthouse, and the coffin was carried inside and laid upon a platform. Over the platform was a canopy of heavy cloth into which had been cut thirty-six stars. The light shone through the stars and fell on the coffin below.

The public viewing began at 5:00 P.M., and by midnight more than forty thousand people had seen Lincoln's corpse.

Jefferson Davis had spent a quiet night in Cokesbury, South Carolina. He left there on May 2 before daylight, and at about 10:00

that morning he rode into Abbeville. The townspeople were happy to see him. Captain William Parker, the officer safeguarding the Confederate treasure wagon train, had arrived before Davis. Parker turned the gold over to John Reagan and allowed the young cadets who had been guarding the treasure to leave for home.

Then Parker called on Davis. "I never saw the President appear to better advantage than during these last hours of the Confederacy," remembered Parker. "He showed no signs of despondency. His air was resolute; and he looked, as he is, a born leader of men."

When Davis heard that Parker had dismissed his band of cadets, he said, "Captain, I am very sorry to hear that," and repeated the words several times. Still hopeful that he could rally the troops, Davis was unhappy about the loss of even a single soldier from the Confederate forces. Parker explained that the secretary of the navy had given the order. "I have no fault to find with you," said Davis, "but I am very sorry Mr. Mallory gave you the order."

Davis suggested that they remain in Abbeville for four days, but Parker warned him that if he stayed that long he would be captured. Davis replied that he would never desert the Southern people. He rose from his chair and began pacing the floor, repeating several times that he would "never abandon his people."

Parker spoke frankly: "Mr. President, if you remain here you will be captured. . . . You will be captured, and you know how we will all feel that." Parker told his president, "It is your duty to the Southern people not to allow yourself to be made a prisoner." He advised Davis on how to escape: "Leave now with a few followers and cross the Mississippi."

Parker was not the only one giving that advice to Davis. On the same day Varina wrote to her husband, worried for his safety. "Do not try to meet me," she told him. "I dread the yankees getting news of you so much, you are the countrys only hope. . . . Why not cut loose from your escort? Go swiftly and alone with the exception of two or three. . . . May God keep you, my old and only love, As ever Devotedly, your own Winnie."

After Davis talked with Parker, he received more bad news. He met with several cavalry officers and asked them about the "condition and spirit" of their men. Were they able and willing to go on fighting?

The answer was discouraging. The officers told him frankly that "they could not depend upon their men for fighting, that they regarded the struggle as over." Davis was again urged by his advisers to make his way quickly to Florida or across the Mississippi, but he still refused. "The idea of personal safety, when the country's condition was before his eyes, was an unpleasant one to him," remembered Stephen Mallory. He was not yet willing to flee for his own life.

Mallory decided that there was nothing more he could do to help Davis. At Abbeville he gave up his job as secretary of the navy. His family needed him, he said, and he did not want to flee the country and abandon them. But he agreed to remain with Davis's party for a few more days.

On May 2 President Andrew Johnson offered a reward of one hundred thousand dollars for Jefferson Davis's capture. The announcement of it accused Davis of being involved in the assassination of Abraham Lincoln.

The first reward poster for Jefferson Davis.

By noon on May 2, the line of people in Chicago waiting to view Lincoln's body stretched nearly a mile. They came all day, and when the doors to the courthouse were shut at 8:00 P.M., the thousands of people still waiting in line had to be turned away. This was a city that felt a special relationship with Abraham Lincoln. He had worked here as a lawyer in the courts; his most famous campaign debates had been held here; and five years ago here he had accepted the nomination to become president. And now, the *Chicago Tribune* newspaper wrote, "he comes back to us, his work finished."

The funeral train left Chicago at 9:30 P.M. The excitement aboard the train increased. This was the last night. In the morning the funeral train would complete its journey, and Lincoln's body would return to Springfield. As the train passed through a town called Lockport, a sign was seen on a house. It read, "Come home."

During the night of May 2 and through the early morning hours of May 3, the residents of Springfield were restless. They had been getting ready for Lincoln's homecoming since they heard news of his death. Now they had finished hanging the decorations and painting the signs. Crepe and bunting blackened the town. Lincoln's own two-story house was a decorated masterpiece of mourning. Over the front door of his law office hung a sign that read, "He Lives in the Hearts of His People."

They had waited eighteen days since Lincoln's death and thirteen days since the train had left Washington. Beginning tomorrow, over the next two days of May 3 and 4, Springfield would show the nation that no town loved Abraham Lincoln more.

CHAPTER TWELVE

That night, more of Jefferson Davis's advisers begged him to flee with a small escort of three officers and make a run for the coast of Florida. Davis, once again, refused. But he did agree to leave Abbeville that night, instead of staying several days.

Davis wrote to Burton Harrison about his plans. The letter was not a happy one, and Davis even expressed his low opinion of the Confederate soldiers and his worry about the Union soldiers hunting for him. "I think all their efforts are directed for my capture and that my family is safest when furthest from me—I have the bitterest disappointment in regard to the feeling of our troops, and would not have any one I loved dependent upon their resistance against an equal force," he wrote.

At 11:00 P.M. Davis left Abbeville. The wagons carrying the Confederate treasury followed, watched over by Secretary of State Benjamin.

★ ★ ★

On the morning of May 3, Lincoln arrived in Springfield. His journey was complete.

Edward Townsend sent his usual matter-of-fact telegram to Stanton: "The funeral train arrived here without accident at 8.40 this morning. The burial is appointed at 12 p.m. to-morrow, Thursday."

Townsend had done it. Under his command, the funeral train had taken the corpse of Abraham Lincoln 1,645 miles from Washington, D.C., to Springfield, Illinois, and it had arrived on schedule. During its thirteen-day journey, the train never broke down, suffered an accident, or left one city a minute late.

At every stop along the way, the soldiers of the honor guard had performed perfectly. Not once did they falter in their handling of the heavy coffin. Whenever they carried the president, whether on level ground, up and down steep winding staircases, or onto a ferryboat, whether in daylight or darkness, in sunshine or a driving rain, the veteran Union army soldiers never made a misstep. Now, in Springfield, they would carry the president of the United States upon their shoulders for the last time.

Lincoln was home, back at the Great Western Railroad Depot where his journey began four years ago, on February 11, 1861. When he left for Washington that morning, he realized that he might never return. He stood in the last car of the train, looked at the faces of his neighbors, and spoke:

> *My friends, no one, not in my situation, can appreciate my feelings of sadness at this parting. To this place, and the kindness of these people, I owe everything. Here I have lived a quarter of a century, and have passed from a young man to an old one. Here my children have been born, and one is buried. I now leave, not*

knowing when, or whether ever, I may return, with a task before
me greater than that which rested upon Washington. Without the
assistance of the Divine Being who ever attended him, I cannot
succeed. With that assistance I cannot fail. Trusting in Him who
can go with me, and remain with you, and be everywhere for good,
let us confidently hope that all will yet be well. To his care com-
mending you, as I hope in your prayers you will commend me, I
bid you an affectionate farewell.

Not long after Lincoln's remains arrived in Springfield, Jefferson Davis arrived in Washington, Georgia. By this time Davis's escort was weary and unhappy. They wanted to go home. John Reagan knew what else they wanted: "Before reaching Washington, [Davis's] cavalry, knowing that they were guarding money, demanded a portion of it," he remembered. If the government failed to pay them, they were going to seize the money. Breckinridge and the officers commanding the cavalry gave in and handed out a portion of the money.

It was in Washington that Judah Benjamin, the secretary of state, decided to leave Davis and make his own escape. The president's pace was too slow for Benjamin's taste, and he thought he would have a better chance to avoid capture on his own. He had never been comfortable riding a horse and set out in a carriage. Reagan spoke to him before he set off and asked where he was going. "To the farthest place from the United States," Benjamin responded, "if it takes me to the middle of China."

Others pushed Jefferson Davis to try to escape, once again urging him to strike out alone or with one companion and get out of the country or over the Mississippi. He responded, "I shall not leave Confederate soil while a Confederate regiment is on it."

In Washington, Georgia, the people welcomed their president as if he rode at the head of a triumphant procession. Eliza Andrews, the twenty-four-year-old daughter of a judge and a plantation owner, described the scene:

"About noon the town was thrown into the wildest excitement by the arrival of President Davis. . . . He rode into town at the head of his escort . . . and as he was passing by the bank . . . several . . . gentlemen were sitting on the front porch, and the instant they recognized him they took off their hats and received him with every mark of respect due the president of a brave people. When he reined in his horse, all the staff who were present advanced to hold the reins and assist him to dismount." This was the warm welcome that Greensboro and Charlotte, North Carolina, had withheld from Davis.

Jefferson Davis, his remaining friends, and soldiers stayed in Washington for a few days. But it could not be long. A letter from Varina and a dispatch from Breckinridge again urged Davis to flee. If he hoped to avoid capture, his advisers were right. Jefferson Davis needed to move fast to the Mississippi River or Florida.

In Springfield the honor guard removed Lincoln's body from the train and took it to the Statehouse, where they laid it on a platform. This morning, for the first time since the funeral train left Washington, the honor guard also removed Willie's coffin from the presidential car.

Springfield was not a great American city, and its people knew they could not hope to rival the displays of Washington, Philadelphia, New York City, or Chicago. Lincoln's hometown even had to borrow a hearse from St. Louis. However, Springfield meant to prove that Abraham Lincoln meant more to his hometown than he did to any other city in the country.

Springfield welcomes Lincoln home.

The embalmer and undertaker opened Lincoln's coffin. He had been dead for eighteen days. Only chemicals and makeup had kept him presentable during the journey. At the beginning, at the White House funeral, Lincoln's face had looked almost natural. He had changed along the way. The face continued to darken, and more and more white face powder had to be applied. Lincoln no longer resembled a sleeping man. Now he looked like a ghastly, pale, waxlike statue.

The doors to the Statehouse opened to the public at 10:00 A.M. on May 3 and stayed that way for twenty-four hours. It was the first round-the-clock viewing since Lincoln had died. During the night trains continued to arrive in Springfield, and people without lodgings wandered the streets until dawn.

By 10:00 A.M. on May 4, seventy-five thousand people had passed by the presidential body. The coffin was removed from the Statehouse and placed in the hearse waiting on Washington Street. The procession began at 11:30 A.M., passing by Lincoln's home, then heading to Oak Ridge Cemetery, about a mile and a half from town. Lincoln's guards removed his coffin from the hearse, carried it into the limestone tomb, and laid it on a marble slab. Willie's coffin rested near him.

The Springfield tomb.

Bishop Matthew Simpson, who had been at the White House funeral, was there to speak. He read the speech that Lincoln had given when he had been sworn in for his second term as president, with its famous lines calling for "malice toward none" and "charity for all." Simpson called for forgiveness of the Southern people: "We will take them to our hearts," he said. But the bishop scorned Jefferson Davis and other Confederate leaders. "Let every man who . . . aided in beginning this rebellion, and thus led to the slaughter of our sons and daughters, be brought to speedy and certain punishment. Let every officer . . . who . . . has turned his sword against . . . his country, be doomed to a felon's death. This . . . is the will of the American people. . . . There shall be no peace to rebels," he declared.

This shocking, tomb-side lust for revenge would have horrified Lincoln.

Lincoln's pastor, the Reverend Dr. Gurley, gave a last prayer, which was followed by a funeral hymn. There was nothing more to say. They closed the iron gates and locked Abraham and Willie Lincoln in their tomb. Then everybody went home.

In Washington, Georgia, a few hundred citizens honored Jefferson Davis on his second day with them. "Crowds of people flocked to see him," wrote Eliza Andrews, "and nearly all were melted to tears." Not only did the townspeople gather around Davis, but they put together an enormous feast. "The village sent so many good things for the President to eat," recalled Eliza, "that an ogre couldn't have devoured them all, and he left many little delicacies . . . to people who had been kind to him."

It was in Washington that Stephen Mallory, the secretary of the navy, left Jefferson Davis. Davis understood that it was time for Mallory to return to his family. He took time to compose a warm farewell letter. Davis did not know it, but it was the last letter he would write as president of the Confederate States of America.

Davis then finally agreed to take the action he should have chosen days ago. He would start south with ten men, his officers, and his secretary, leaving Breckinridge to finish up any business of the War Department and John Reagan to handle anything dealing with the Post-office Department or the Treasury.

Eliza Andrews watched Davis ride out the night of May 4. She had heard rumors that the Union army did not actually want to capture Davis: "The general belief is that Grant and the military men, even Sherman, are not anxious for the ugly job of hanging such a man as our president, and are quite willing to let him give them the slip, and get out of the country if he can. The military men, who do the hard and cruel things in war, seem to be more merciful in peace than the politicians who stay at home and do the talking."

For the past three weeks, the newspapers had told the story of Lincoln's last journey. Every stop of the train, every city it passed through, every person who marched in the processions, every detail of the black drapery and silver trim and lavish flowers that decorated the hearses and the viewing chambers—no detail was too unimportant for the papers to print or for people to read.

It was impossible for everyone in the country to hurry to Washington, D.C., for the procession, funeral, and viewing there or to go to the cities where the funeral train would stop. These stories carried every American who read them to Lincoln's side and allowed them to imagine what it must have been like to behold his face or

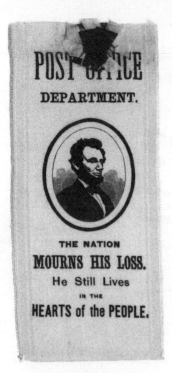

POST OFFICE
DEPARTMENT.

THE NATION
MOURNS HIS LOSS.
He Still Lives
IN THE
HEARTS of the PEOPLE.

Mourning ribbon worn in
Washington by Post Office
workers for the April 19, 1865,
funeral procession.

to watch his coffin pass by. Newspapers made it possible for the American people to ride aboard that train.

As they viewed Lincoln's corpse, watched his funeral train pass by, or eagerly read the newspaper stories, Americans mourned the death of their president. They honored his achievements: He had won the war, saved the Union, and set men free. They vowed to bear the burden of his unfinished work. And they declared, by the tributes they paid to him, that his great cause was worth fighting and dying for.

For whom did all these people mourn? For their dead president, of course. But this outpouring of sorrow was not for just one man. They mourned for all the men—every son, every brother, every husband, and every father—lost in that war. It was as though, on that train, in that coffin, they were *all* coming home.

CHAPTER THIRTEEN

On the day that Lincoln was at last buried, more than sixteen hundred miles away in Washington, D.C., offices were closed, public buildings were still draped in black, and flags flew at half staff. Army officers wore black crepe ribbons around their coat sleeves. John Wilkes Booth lay in a secret, unmarked grave on the grounds of the United States Army penitentiary. Booth's coconspirators awaited trial. Secretary of State Seward was recovering from his wounds.

At the White House Abraham Lincoln's office was still just as the president left it on the afternoon of April 14. His widow was still living there. She had refused to leave, which meant that the new president, Andrew Johnson, could not move in. It had become the subject of much talk. At the Petersen house Private William Clarke went to bed each night covered by the same quilt that had warmed the dying president.

Now Secretary of War Edwin M. Stanton could focus his attention on the capture of Jefferson Davis. Lincoln's journey was over at last. But Jefferson Davis still had further to go.

On May 5 Jefferson Davis and the small group of men still traveling with him made a camp near Sandersville, Georgia. The next day Burton Harrison directed Varina Davis and the train of wagons carrying her property to camp off the road near Dublin, Georgia. Around midnight Davis's party stumbled upon her campsite. More than a month had gone by since Davis had seen his family. They traveled together on May 7.

On May 7 Lieutenant Colonel Benjamin Pritchard, commanding the Fourth Michigan Cavalry regiment, left Macon, Georgia, in pursuit of Jefferson Davis. His orders were to capture or kill him.

On May 8 Davis separated from his family again. At dawn he rode on. By nightfall he had made little progress through heavy rains, and Varina's train caught up with him. Before dawn on May 9 they were together once more.

Lieutenant Colonel Pritchard and his men arrived at Abbeville, Georgia, at 3:00 P.M. on May 9. There he encountered the commander of the First Wisconsin Cavalry, who told Pritchard that a wagon train had crossed the Ocmulgee River the night before, a mile and a half north of Abbeville.

The Wisconsin men went off down the main road while Pritchard's soldiers planned to follow the river. Pritchard left Abbeville at 4:00 P.M., headed toward Irwinville.

Toward the end of the day on May 9, Davis decided to make camp for the night with Varina's wagon train near Irwinville. They pulled off the road, and pine trees helped conceal their position. The tents and wagons were scattered over an area of about one hundred yards. Any Yankee who rode into one part of the camp during the night would not be able to see to the other side of it. Davis, unless captured at once, could escape into the woods under the cover of darkness. The layout was perfect, except for one flaw. Despite two dangers—thieves looking for plunder and the Union cavalry hunting for Davis—they posted no guards to keep watch.

When Jefferson Davis entered his wife's tent late on the night of May 9, 1865, he was lucky to still be a free man. Davis's advisers knew that it was too dangerous for the president to continue traveling with his wife's slow-moving wagon train. Unless Davis left his family and moved fast on horseback, along with just three or four men, he had little chance of escape.

Davis said that on the night of May 9 he would eat dinner, stay up late, and leave on horseback under cover of darkness. He was dressed for the road: dark felt, wide-brimmed hat; wool frock coat of Confederate gray; gray trousers; high, black leather riding boots and spurs. His horse was tied near Varina's tent, already saddled, with his saddle holsters loaded with Davis's pistols, ready to ride.

Several of the men, including John Reagan, stayed up late talking, waiting for Davis to give the order to depart. It never came. The delay puzzled one of the men picked to accompany the president. "Time wore on, the afternoon was spent, night set in, and we were still in camp," he wrote later. "Why the order 'to horse' was not given by the President I do not know."

Pritchard's men arrived in Irwinville at 1:00 A.M. on May 10, but found no traces of Davis or his followers. Pritchard rode ahead with a few men and, posing as Confederate cavalrymen, they questioned some villagers. The locals told Pritchard that at sunset a party with wagons had camped a mile, or a mile and a half, from town out on the Abbeville road.

Pritchard positioned his men about half a mile from the mysterious encampment. He sent twenty-five men, guided by a local black man and under the command of Lieutenant Alfred Purington, to circle around the camp and cut off any chance of escape from the rear. He waited for daylight. He didn't want any of the Confederates to escape into the woods under cover of darkness.

For the next hour and a half, they waited in the dark.

At 3:30 A.M., at the first hint of dawn, Pritchard ordered his men into their saddles and to ride forward. After a quick dash, they succeeded in capturing the camp and everyone in it. Pritchard's men had not fired a shot. "The surprise was so complete," Pritchard wrote later, "that few of the enemy were enabled to make the slightest defense, or even arouse from their slumbers in time to grasp their weapons, which were lying at their sides, before they were wholly in our power."

But before Pritchard's men could gain full control, and before the colonel was even sure that he had captured Jefferson Davis's camp, gunfire broke out. It came from behind the camp, where Pritchard had sent Lieutenant Purington and his twenty-five men. It was a rebel counterattack, Pritchard assumed. He spurred his horse past the tents and wagons and rode to the sound of the fighting.

Lieutenant Purington and the men under his command were in position behind Davis's camp, waiting for Pritchard's signal. As Purington faced Davis's camp, he heard mounted men approaching him from his rear. They called out that they were "friends." But they refused to identify themselves and would not ride forward when Purington ordered them to. One of them shouted, "By God, you are the men we are looking for," and began to ride away. Purington ordered his men to open fire.

In the dark the two groups of armed men could not see that they wore the same uniform, Union blue cavalry shell jackets decorated with bright yellow piping. The Fourth Michigan Cavalry was fighting the First Wisconsin.

The gunfire woke the people in Jefferson Davis's camp, and one man sounded the alarm. "I was awakened by the coachman, Jim Jones," Burton Harrison remembered, "running to me about day-break with the announcement that the enemy was at hand!" Harrison drew his pistol and faced several men from the Fourth Michigan charging up the road from the south. He raised his weapon and took aim.

"As soon as one of them came within range," Harrison said, "I covered him with my revolver and was about to fire, but lowered the weapon when I perceived the attacking column was so strong as to make resistance useless, and reflected that, by killing the man, I should certainly not be helping ourselves. . . . We were taken by surprise, and not one of us exchanged a shot with the enemy."

John Reagan, the postmaster general, was there as well. "The major of the regiment reached the place where I and the members of the President's staff were camped," he said later. "When he approached me I was watching a struggle between two federal soldiers and Governor Lubbock. They were trying to get his horse and saddle bags away from him and he was holding on to them and refusing to give them up; they threatened to shoot him if he did not, and he replied . . . that they might shoot and be damned, but that they should not rob him while he was alive and looking on."

Jefferson Davis, still inside Varina's tent, had received his coach-man's warning. He now heard the gunfire and the horses in the camp. He assumed that the riders were Confederate deserters, thieves plan-ning to rob Mrs. Davis's wagon train. "Those men have attacked us at last," he warned his wife. "I will go out and see if I cannot stop the firing; surely I still have some authority with the Confederates." Upon going to the tent door, however, he saw the blue coats of the Union soldiers and turned to Varina. "The Federal cavalry are upon us," he told her.

Davis had not undressed during the night. He needed no time to get ready. His pistols and saddled horse were within sight of the tent. If he could get to that horse, he could leap into the saddle and gallop for the woods. He was still a superb rider and must have felt that he could outride any Yankee cavalryman half his age. Seconds, not minutes, counted now, and if he hoped to escape he had to act at once.

Before he left, Varina asked him to wear an overcoat, also known as a "waterproof." It was cool and drizzling, and if he could escape the camp, he faced several hours of hard riding. The extra layer of warmth might help, and the coat might also conceal his identity. "Knowing he would be recognized," Varina explained, "I plead with him to let me throw over him a large waterproof which had often served him in sickness during the summer as a dressing gown, and which I hoped might so cover his person that in the grey of the morn-ing he would not be recognized. As he strode off I threw over his head a little black shawl which was round my own shoulders, seeing that he could not find his hat." These two garments—the coat and shawl—would help create a myth that Davis had attempted to evade capture by wearing women's clothing.

Jefferson Davis described what happened next. "I had gone

JEFF DAVIS,
AS HE APPEARED WHEN CAPTURED.

Popular images lampooned Davis
for allegedly attempting to escape
capture dressed as a woman.

perhaps between fifteen or twenty yards when a trooper galloped up and ordered me to halt and surrender, to which I gave a defiant answer, and, dropping the shawl and the raglan from my shoulders, advanced toward him." The soldier leveled his weapon at Davis, but the Confederate president did not hesitate. "But I expected, if he fired, he would miss me, and my intention was in that event to put my hand under his foot, tumble him off on the other side, spring into the saddle, and attempt to escape. My wife, who had been watching me, when she saw the soldier aim his **carbine** at me, ran forward and threw her arms around me. . . . Recognizing that the opportunity had been lost, I turned back, and, the morning being damp and chilly, passed on to a fire beyond the tent. . . ."

The manhunt was over. Jefferson Davis and everyone with him had been captured. But the gunfire was still going on. One of Davis's men warned Pritchard that if shots were being fired, it was not the Confederates being killed. "Captain, your men are fighting each other over yonder," he said.

Pritchard was sure that Davis's camp must be protected by more soldiers. But the other man insisted that he was wrong. "You have our whole camp; I know your men are fighting each other," he said.

Soon Pritchard and his officers discovered it was true. There were no Confederate soldiers behind the camp, only two Union regiments—the Fourth Michigan and the First Wisconsin. All were attempting to earn the glory of capturing Jefferson Davis and the gold he was supposed to have with him. Every Union soldier had heard the rumors—the "rebel chief" was fleeing with millions of dollars in gold coins. Yes, Confederate treasure was on the move in April and May 1865, but what the manhunters did not know was that Jefferson Davis was not the one transporting it.

The gun battle caused hard feelings between the two regiments. They blamed each other and fought over the reward money promised to whoever captured Davis. The Fourth Michigan wanted to

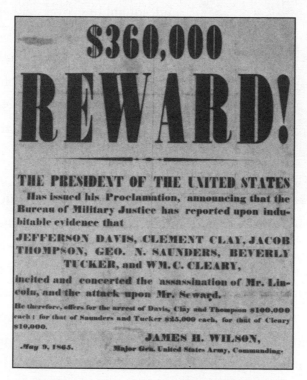

A second reward poster for Davis and other
Confederate leaders. Neither Davis nor his pursuers
learned of the reward until after he was captured.

On the morning of his capture, Jefferson Davis wore a suit of Confederate gray and not one of Varina's hoop skirts.

claim all the money and did not want to share it with the First Wisconsin. The Wisconsin men complained that if the Fourth had not fired upon them, then they would have been the ones who would have captured Davis.

Jefferson Davis, who sacrificed all he had for the Confederacy and who was captured penniless, without a single dollar to his name, must have appreciated the irony. He never commented about it, but it surely amused him to see Yankees killing each other and squabbling over money in their zeal to claim him as their prize.

It was not until the skirmish between two regiments of the same army was over that Colonel Pritchard became aware that he had captured the president of the Confederate States of America.

The men traveling with the president had used good judgment on the morning of May 10. No matter how much they desired to open fire on the Union cavalry, they knew they would lose the fight. They might kill several of the enemy, but the Union soldiers, outnumbering them by more than ten to one, might kill them all and then shoot the president. A

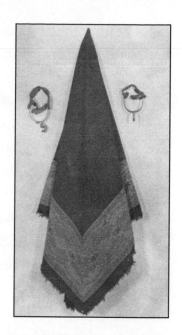

Truth vs. Myth. Left: The Raglan coat Jefferson Davis actually wore the morning of his capture. Right: The shawl and spurs Davis wore the morning of May 10, 1865.

gunfight at dawn, when visibility was low, might also lead to the deaths of Mrs. Davis and the children. Surrender, however hateful, was the honorable choice.

And so, thirty-eight days after he left Richmond, after a journey through four states by railroad, ferryboat, horse, and wagon, Jefferson Davis was a prisoner. Several of his supporters thought he could have evaded the manhunt and made it all the way to Mexico, Texas, Cuba, or Europe, if only he had placed his own safety ahead of his own wish to continue to fight for the cause and preserve the Confederacy.

No one is sure why Jefferson Davis did not leave the camp that night. Perhaps he was tired. Perhaps he hoped a few more hours of stolen rest would not matter. Perhaps he thought it was too late to escape to Texas. Perhaps he believed that, once he left this camp, he would never see his wife and children again. Perhaps part of him did not want to flee, run away to another country, and vanish from history. We will never know.

Davis failed in his mission. He did not rally the Confederate army or the Southern people to continue the war. He did not escape to Texas to create a new Confederacy across the Mississippi River. But he had done his best. Robert E. Lee once said: "No man could have done better."

The war, and the manhunt for Jefferson Davis, were over. But he was alive. May 10, 1865, was the end for Jefferson Davis's country and his presidency. Now Davis would begin a new, twelve-day journey to prison.

That day in the Union capital, people did not rush into the streets to celebrate Davis's capture. No one knew about it. Georgia was too far away for the news to travel to Washington on the same day. Instead, the newspapers were still filled with headlines and stories about the Lincoln assassination. May 10 was the opening day of the trial for the seven men and one woman accused of being accomplices in John Wilkes Booth's plot to murder Abraham Lincoln and Secretary Seward. Many people believed that if Davis were captured before the trial ended, he would be rushed to Washington and charged as the ninth conspirator in Lincoln's murder.

On the morning of their capture on May 10, Davis, his family, and his aides remained defiant. They were not meek prisoners. They objected to the soldiers plundering their belongings, were offended at the disrespectful way the soldiers addressed the president, and scorned their captors as inferiors. To the Southern mind, these

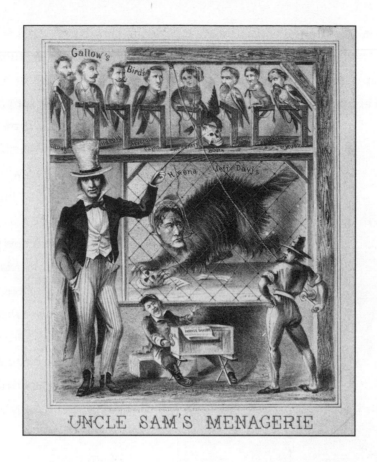

UNCLE SAM'S MENAGERIE

This fanciful print depicts Davis as a caged hyena wearing
a lady's bonnet. The Lincoln assassination conspirators
perch above him on gallows, foreshadowing their execution.

rude, ungentlemanly, thieving Yankee troops represented all that was
wrong with the North.

Their Southern pride infuriated their captors. The cavalrymen
would find a way to settle the score, not with violence but by attacking Jefferson Davis's most precious possession—his reputation. This
was the beginning of the myth that Jefferson Davis was captured in

women's clothing—a myth that is repeated to this day.

"The foolish and wicked charge was made that he was captured in woman's clothes," John Reagan wrote indignantly. "He was also pictured as having bags of gold on him when captured. . . . I saw him a few minutes after his surrender, wearing his accustomed suit of Confederate gray, with his boots and hat on . . . and he had no money."

Davis and his fellow prisoners were taken to Macon, Georgia. From there, on May 14, Davis was taken by train to Atlanta, and then he traveled to Augusta, from where he departed for Savannah.

"JEFF. DAVIS AND HIS LAST DITCH."
Entered according to act of Congress in the year 1865, by J. BRILL, in the Clerk's Office of the District Court, for the Southern District of New York.

Another popular image that lampooned Davis for allegedly attempting to escape capture dressed as a woman.

CHAPTER FOURTEEN

On Sunday, May 14, a month after the assassination of Abraham Lincoln and ten days after his burial in Springfield, the citizens of Washington read their morning papers and learned stupendous news. Jefferson Davis had been taken. "Thank God we have got the arch traitor at last," Benjamin Brown French wrote in his diary. "I hope he will not be suffered to escape or commit suicide. Hanging will be too good for him."

While some hoped to see Jefferson Davis die, others hoped to make a profit out of his capture—particularly the circus owner P. T. Barnum. Barnum owned the American Museum in New York City, full of treasures and curiosities. As soon as he heard the story that Jefferson Davis had been captured in a dress, he wanted it as an exhibit. He wrote to Stanton, offering to make a donation to either the care of wounded soldiers or the care of freed slaves if he could have that dress.

Stanton said no. He planned to keep the gown for himself. But

Now therefore I, Jefferson Davis,
President of the Confederate States of America,—
all I want is to be let alone!

Entered according to Act of Congress, in the year 1865, by B. LEVERETT
EMERSON, in the Clerk's office of the District Court for the District of
Massachusetts   129 Washington St. Boston.

**Printmakers continued to ridicule Davis
after his capture.**

once the clothes worn by Davis during his capture arrived in Washington, Stanton saw that the story was a huge exaggeration. The "dress" was a loose-fitting, waterproof "raglan," or overcoat. The "bonnet" was a rectangular shawl, a type of wrap President Lincoln had worn on chilly evenings. But the story continued to be told, and drawings, cartoons, and prints all over the country showed Davis in a hoopskirt and a bonnet.

On May 16 Davis arrived in Savannah, Georgia, where he was put aboard a vessel bound for Fortress Monroe, Virginia. Meanwhile, Edwin Stanton was trying to decide what should be done with some prisoners he did not want—Varina Davis and the women who had been arrested with her. He discussed the question with Gideon Welles and General Grant. Stanton exclaimed that the women must be "sent off" because "we did not want them." "They must go South," he declared. Welles could not resist toying with him. "The South is very indefinite, and you permit them to select the place. Mrs. Davis may designate Norfolk, or Richmond." Or anywhere.

Stanton could not stand the idea of the former First Lady of the

Confederacy showing up wherever she wanted. "Stanton was annoyed," Welles saw, and "I think, altered the telegram." Stanton suspected that if Varina returned to Washington, she could be a dangerous political opponent.

By Monday, May 22, Jefferson Davis was imprisoned in Fortress Monroe, Virginia. He did not know whether he would ever see his wife and children again or even how long he would live. When he parted with Varina, he told her not to cry. It would, he said, only make the Yankees gloat.

His captors refused to address him as "Mr. President." They called him "Jeffy," "the rebel chieftain," or "the state prisoner." He was always watched, and often not allowed to sleep. Through insult, isolation, and silence, they tried to humiliate him and break his spirit. He was, in the words of some newspapers, the arch criminal of the age, a man "buried

Within days of his capture, popular prints ridiculed the Confederate president.

alive" who must never be set free. Many people hoped that he would never emerge from his dungeon alive.

Shortly after he was shut inside his prison, men entered Davis's cell and told him they had orders to shackle him. Davis saw the blacksmith with his tools and chains. He told them all that he refused to allow such a humiliation, pointed to the officer in charge, and said he would have to kill him first. Davis dared his jailers to shoot him.

Soldiers lunged forward to grab him, but Davis knocked one man aside and kicked another away with his boot. Then several ganged up on him, seized him, and held him down while the smith locked the chains in place.

Printmakers continued to ridicule Davis after his imprisonment.

Contemporary sketch of Davis in his cell at Fortress Monroe.

As Davis entered prison, Mary Lincoln at last moved out of the White House. Benjamin Brown French, the commissioner of public buildings and grounds, went to say good-bye. "Mrs. Mary Lincoln left the City on Monday evening at 6 o'clock, with her sons Robert & Tad (Thomas)," he wrote. "I went up and bade her good-by, and felt really very sad, although she has given me a world of trouble. I think the sudden and awful death of the President somewhat unhinged her mind, for at times she has exhibited all the symptoms of madness. . . . It is not proper that I should write down, *even here*, all I know! May God have her in his keeping, and make her a better woman. That is my sincere wish. . . ."

By May 24 Lincoln's home in Springfield was no longer a center of the nation's attention. But on this day a photographer—no one knows who—showed up to take the last known picture of the Lincoln home draped in mourning. The black bunting was wind-swept and weather-beaten. It was the same all across the nation. People could not bear to take down their wind-tattered, sun-faded, and rain-streaked decorations of death and mourning. Better, many thought, to allow time and nature to sweep them away.

After the funeral, the last photograph of Lincoln's
Springfield home draped in mourning, May 24, 1865.

On July 7, 1865, four of those who had helped John Wilkes Booth in his plot to murder Lincoln were executed. Three were sentenced to life in prison. But their trial had made one thing clear—Jefferson Davis had played no part in the assassination of Abraham Lincoln. If Davis was to be put on trial or executed, it would be for treason, not for the president's murder.

After several weeks of silence, Varina received her first letter from Davis since his capture. It was written on the twenty-first of August. "Kiss the Baby for me," he wrote. "My dear Wife, equally the centre of my love and confidence, remember how good the Lord has always been to me, how often he has wonderfully preserved me, and put thy trust in Him."

Davis and Varina wrote many letters to each other while he was in prison, and she was not the only person he received letters from. On January 29, 1866, a young girl in Richmond, Emily Jessie Morton, wrote to Davis to cheer him up.

"I hope that you will not think me a rude little girl to takeing the liberty of writing to you, but I want to tell you how much I love you, and how sorry I feel for you to be kept so long in Prison away from your dear little children. . . . I go to school to Mrs. Mumford where there are upwards of thirty scholars all of which love you very much and are taught to do so. When we go to Hollywood [cemetery] to decorate our dear soldiers graves on the 31st of May your little Joes grave will not be forgotten."

On May 3, 1866, Varina Davis arrived at Fortress Monroe. She brought her baby daughter, Varina Anne, but left her other children behind. Her misson now was to save her husband's life. Varina had been a popular and well-liked figure in Washington before the war. Now she used every social and political skill she had learned to save her husband. She wrote letters, met with important people, and talked to the newspapers. And eventually it began to work.

By the fall of 1866, the government had still not put Jefferson Davis on trial for treason. Davis welcomed the idea of a trial. If he was found innocent, then the South was not wrong—it did have the right to leave the Union. If he was found guilty, he was happy to suffer on behalf of his people. His death, he believed, would win mercy for the South.

The U.S. government wanted neither result. If a federal court said that it was *not* treason for some states to try to become a separate country, that would overturn the whole purpose and result of the war. But if Davis was found guilty and executed, he would become a martyr and inspire the South to fight back.

Davis stayed in prison through the winter of 1867. But by the spring the government finally decided that it wanted Davis off its hands. He would be released on bail. The government claimed the right to put him on trial at a later time, if they chose, but they would not do so now.

At 7:00 A.M. on May 11, 1867, the former Confederate president, still a prisoner, left Fortress Monroe and boarded a steamboat for Richmond. At 6:00 P.M. Davis reached the city, landing in the same place where, two years ago, Abraham Lincoln had received a wild welcome from the city's slaves. Now the white citizens welcomed Davis back to his old capital. As he passed, men uncovered their heads and women waved handkerchiefs. "I feel like an unhappy ghost visiting this much beloved city," Jefferson told Varina.

On May 13 Davis appeared in court, his supporters posted a bail of a hundred thousand dollars, and he was freed. He was never tried, never convicted of treason, or of any crime. Once free, his first act was one of remembrance. He brought flowers to the grave of his son Joseph Evan Davis at Hollywood Cemetery, and while there he also decorated graves of Confederate soldiers.

On June 1 a Confederate officer who had served under President Davis sent him a heartfelt letter, which rejoiced in Davis's freedom. "Your release has lifted a load from my heart which I have not words to tell," it said, "and my daily prayer to the great Ruler of the World, is that he may shield you from all future harm, guard you from all evil, and give you the peace which the world can not take away. That the rest of your days may be triumphantly happy, is the sincere and earnest wish of your most obedient faithful friend and servant." The letter was signed by Robert E. Lee.

After his release, Davis was forced to ask himself questions. What did the future hold? Where would he go? What would he do? How would he live? How would he earn money? Like much of the South, his life was in ruins. He had lost everything. His plantation was wrecked, no crops grew there, and he owned no slaves to work the fields. Union soldiers had looted his Mississippi home of everything valuable. They even stole his love letters from Sarah Knox Taylor.

Davis also had to decide what *not* to do. He vowed to do nothing to bring dishonor upon himself, his people, or the Confederacy. Because so many Southerners were poor, he decided that he would not shame himself by accepting charity while others were in need. He would not speak publicly against the Union, out of fear that his words might cause his people to be punished. He would not run in any election. He knew without doubt that he could be elected to any position in the South. But to run he would have to take a loyalty oath to the

Oil portrait of Jefferson Davis as he appeared in the 1870s.

Union, something he would never do. To swear that oath, to say seces-sion was wrong, would betray every soldier who had laid down his life for the cause. He would rather suffer death. And lastly, he decided he would never return to Washington, D.C.

Davis tried a few jobs but did not have much success. He found his true calling in a new role: remembering and honoring the Confederacy and those who had died for its cause. He wrote articles and letters, answering countless questions about how the war had been fought. He read histories of the war written by generals and political leaders. He supported the creation of the Southern Historical Association.

During the years following his release from prison, Davis did not have a permanent place to live. In 1877 a friend invited Davis to visit her estate in Mississippi, Beauvoir, near Biloxi. When the owner died, she left the house to him in her will and it became his home. Davis seemed destined for a quiet life at Beauvoir: receiving guests,

On the front porch at Beauvoir.

dining with friends, writing letters, and sitting on the veranda, enjoying the sea breezes. It was there that he finished writing a book about the Confederacy, which was published in 1881: *Rise and Fall of the Confederate Government.*

Then an invitation came. In 1886 Jefferson Davis agreed to make a speaking tour, giving speeches in several cities in the South.

When he boarded the train, he could not have known that he would return from this trip a different man. He did not know that by the end of this journey, more than two decades after the end of the war, the South would love him more than it ever did.

On April 28 Davis, seventy-nine years old, arrived in Montgomery, Alabama. He had no idea what kind of reception he would receive. When he rose and began to speak, no one could hear him. The sound of thousands of cheering voices drowned him out. "Brethren," Davis cried out. That single word—"brethren"—made the crowd shout even louder. Women stood on their chairs and, weeping and laughing from joy, flapped their handkerchiefs like little signal flags. Then the audience allowed him to speak.

Davis spoke of the war, of watching the young men of Alabama march bravely off to combat. "But they are not dead," he told the crowd. "The spirit of Southern liberty is not dead. . . . I have been promised, my friends, that I should not be called upon to make a speech, and therefore I will only extend my heartfelt thanks. God bless you, one and all, men and boys, and the ladies above all others, who never faltered in our direst need." His remarks done, Jefferson Davis sat down.

What happened next stunned the reporter from the *Atlanta Constitution*: "Such a cheer as followed the speaker to his seat cannot be described. It was from the heart. It was an outburst of nature. It was long continued. Mr. Davis got up again and bowed. . . . Men went wild for him; women were in ecstasy for him; children caught the spirit and waved their hands in the air." Widows dressed in black collapsed at his feet. Confederate veterans, many missing arms or legs, and wearing their old uniforms, trembled at his touch.

Everywhere he went on his tour, he received the same kind of welcome. Southerners gathered along the tracks to watch his train fly by, just as Northerners had gathered more than twenty years before to watch for Abraham Lincoln's funeral train. At every platform crowds thronged. Jefferson Davis was more popular than ever.

After the tour Davis returned to Beauvoir. On June 3, 1888, he celebrated his eightieth birthday. Abraham Lincoln was only fifty-six when he was assassinated, and he had no time to savor his victory. Jefferson Davis had had twenty-three years to reflect upon his defeat. From all across the South, from people high and low, congratulations and gifts for Davis poured in.

One letter, from a former Confederate soldier, spoke for all the veterans who had survived the war. "As a native of Ponotoc, Miss., and as an ex-confederate, who entered the army at 17 years of age and remained till the last gun had fired, may I not claim a few moments of your time by tendering to you my congratulations on this your eightieth birthday?" the soldier wrote. "All of us are indeed proud that you have been permitted to remain with us until the ripe age of eighty and we pray earnestly that you may be permitted to enjoy many more years of health, happiness and prosperity. . . ."

But Jefferson Davis did not have many more years. He died one year later, in New Orleans, peacefully, with his wife's hands folded into his.

Jefferson Davis lies in state in New Orleans.

There was a magnificent funeral in New Orleans, and Davis was buried at Metairie Cemetery. But everyone knew this was only a temporary resting place. It was understood that Varina Davis would select a permanent gravesite. Several states, including Mississippi, fought for the honor. In 1891 Varina chose Virginia. Davis would return to his capital city, Richmond.

In 1893 Davis's body was placed aboard a funeral train bound for Virginia. To those who remembered 1865, the sight of another presidential train winding its way through the nation was familiar

The New Orleans funeral procession.

and eerie. In Richmond a grand procession escorted the remains to Hollywood Cemetery.

Jefferson Davis had survived Abraham Lincoln by twenty-four years. Now, his journey also done, he joined him in the grave.

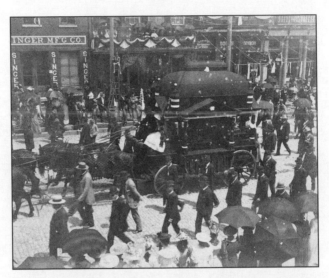

The Raleigh, North Carolina, funeral procession, on the way to Richmond.

Floral tribute at the Raleigh ceremonies.

EPILOGUE

The chase for Jefferson Davis and the death pageant for Abraham Lincoln are among the great American journeys. Like the explorations of Lewis and Clark, the settling of the West, the building of the transcontinental railroad, and the landing on the moon, the rise and fall of the two Civil War presidents, each a martyr to his cause, altered our history and added to our myths. The history is well known—620,000 dead, the overthrow of old ways of life, and the end of a great but flawed antebellum empire built upon slavery. When Lincoln and Davis fell from power, they also set in motion two myths—the legend of America's emancipating, secular saint, and the legend of the Lost Cause. The assassination, nationwide mourning, and funeral for Lincoln; and the chase, imprisonment, and long Civil War afterlife of Davis haunt American history down to the latest generation.

★ ★ ★

In the years following Lincoln's funeral, the melancholy curse that afflicted his family would not lift. During the months after Mary left Washington, there were rumors that she had plundered the White House of valuables; and in 1867, a scheme she hatched with her friend Elizabeth Keckly to exhibit her dresses for money—the "old clothes scandal," as the press dubbed it—made her a national laughingstock. Tad, the president's constant companion after Willie's death, died of tuberculosis in 1871 when he was eighteen, having survived his father by just six years. The body of another Lincoln was put aboard a train. The tomb in Springfield was opened, and Tad joined Abraham, Willie, and Eddie. Mary continued to live as an unsettled wanderer and spent much of her time in Europe. Irrationally, she believed herself destitute. She made mad, vicious accusations of dishonesty and theft against her son Robert, which led him to have her committed to a sanitarium for four months in 1875. She posed for the notorious spirit photographer Mumler, who supplied her with the expected image of the ghosts of Abraham and Willie hovering above her. She finally returned to Springfield and moved into the home of her sister, Elizabeth Todd Edwards. It was the house she and Abraham had been married in. As she had after the assassination, Mary spent much time in seclusion in her room, longing for death. She died on July 16, 1882, surviving her husband by seventeen unhappy years. She joined her family in the tomb. The nation did not mourn her passing. Robert Todd Lincoln became a prominent attorney, businessman, and government official, but after his death in 1926, the Lincoln line died out within two generations. Today there are no direct descendants of Abraham Lincoln.

Varina Davis went on to live a fulfilling life after Jefferson's death. She helped plan his funeral and took pride in how the South mourned him. In 1893, Varina oversaw her husband's reburial in Richmond. In 1890, Varina published her book *Jefferson Davis, Ex-President of the Confederate States of America, a Memoir, by His Wife*. Jefferson had dedicated his memoirs to the women of the Confederacy, and in hers Varina remembered the men: "To the soldiers of the Confederacy, who cheered and sustained Jefferson Davis in the darkest hour by their splendid gallantry, and never withdrew their confidence from him when defeat settled on our cause, this volume is affectionately dedicated. . . ." Like her husband, she needed two fat volumes to tell her story. Unlike him, she unburdened her heart.

In 1891 Varina moved to New York City, a decision that confused many Southerners and disappointed others. While she left behind the Southern landscape of her past, she did not abandon her memories of it. She wrote articles, made new friends, maintained a literary salon, and created a Manhattan Confederate circle that included Burton Harrison, who had become a prominent lawyer, and his wife, Constance Cary Harrison. They, too, wrote about their lives and times in the old Confederacy. Varina Howell Davis died in 1906. All of her sons had preceded Jefferson in death, but through her daughter, Margaret, the family line lived on, and today the direct descendants of Jefferson and Varina Davis work to preserve the memory of their ancestors.

Little physical evidence of the Lincoln funeral train survives. The steam engines that performed flawlessly during the sixteen-hundred-mile journey were scrapped long ago. In 1866 the presidential car was auctioned and purchased by the Union Pacific Railroad. Afterward, the president's funeral car enjoyed a few decades of celebrity but then, stripped of its decorations and furniture and suffering from neglect and decay, it perished in a fire. Souvenir photo postcards from the day depict a pile of collapsed, wooden ribs charred black. The other coach cars vanished, and the funeral train survives only in the dozens of photographs that were taken of it along the route from Washington to Springfield.

None of the majestic horse-drawn hearses, which had once caused the public to marvel at their size and extravagance, exists today. All of the catafalques save one—the one upon which Lincoln's coffin rested when he lay in state at the U.S. Capitol, and upon which dead presidents still repose—are gone. From all the hearses and catafalques, only a few relics survive, scattered among historical societies and private collections: framed slivers of wood, swatches of black cloth, frayed bits of flag, strips of silver fringe, bullion tassels, dried flowers, and the like. From the New York City funeral, one of the twelve halberd-topped flagpoles mounted to Lincoln's hearse survives, preserved by the assistant undertaker and identified for future generations by his sworn affidavit.

Not long after the funeral train left Springfield and returned to Washington, a legend spread of a Lincoln ghost train that rolled down the tracks each spring. An undated, fugitive newspaper clipping, found pasted in an old scrapbook from the late 1860s, is the only surviving evidence of the tale:

A Phantom Train

The Dead Lincoln's Yearly Trip over the New York Central Railroad

A correspondent in the Albany (N.Y.) *Evening Times* relates a conversation with a superstitious night watchman on the New York Central Railroad. Said the watchman: "I believe in spirits and ghosts. I know such things exist. If you will come up in April I will convince you." He then told of the phantom train that every year comes up the road with the body of Abraham Lincoln. Regularly in the month of April, about midnight, the air on the track becomes very keen and cutting. On either side it is warm and still. Every watchman when he feels this air steps off the track and sits down to watch. Soon after the pilot engine, with long black streamers, and a band of black instruments, playing dirges, grinning skeletons sitting all about, will pass up noiselessly, and the very air grows black. If it is moonlight clouds always come over the moon, and the music seems to linger, as if frozen with horror. A few moments after and the phantom train glides by. Flags and streamers hang about. The track ahead seems covered with black carpet, and the wheels are draped with the same. The coffin of the murdered Lincoln is seen lying on the center of the car, and all about it in the air and the train behind are vast numbers of blue-coated men, some with coffins on their backs, others leaning on them.

Many spirits, claimed the storyteller, accompanied Lincoln:

It seems then that all the vast armies that died during the war are escorting the phantom train of the President. The wind, if blowing, dies away at once, and all over the earth a solemn hush, almost stifling, prevails. If a train were passing, its noise would be drowned in silence, and the phantom train would ride over it. Clocks and watches would always stop, and when looked at are found to be from five to eight minutes behind. Everywhere on the road, about the 27th of April, the time of watches and trains is found suddenly behind. This, said the leading watchman, was from the passage of the phantom train.

More tangible than any alleged ghost trains are the railroad tracks. For the most part, the route followed by the Lincoln funeral train still exists, marked by ancient railroad beds and the villages, towns, and cities on the map when the train passed by. Yes, the aging iron rails forged by the Civil War were replaced long ago, but track locations rarely change, and many of the same railroad beds over which Lincoln's coffin rode are still in the same place, a hundred and fifty years later. Few of the residents who live along the route today know about the torches, bonfires, arches, cannon fire, and huge crowds, or that Lincoln's corpse once passed that way and perhaps even stopped in their town. Every day in America, thousands of railroad passengers, unbeknownst to them, follow the route of the funeral train.

Other vivid and more venerated evidence of the death pageant survives; namely, the blood relics—locks of Lincoln's hair, tiny pieces of his skull, the probe and other medical instruments, bloodstained pillows and towels, the physicians' bloody shirt cuffs; the fatal bullet, of course; and still more death relics, lurid and macabre ones, best not spoken of. Many of them repose in the Army Medical Museum or in private collections, handed down from generation to generation or sold off by the descendants of the ancestors who had once cherished them.

More common than blood relics are the ribbons, timetables, badges, song sheets, broadsides, prints, and photographs that were produced and sold commercially to millions of mourners of April and May 1865. Even today, it is not unheard of for a silk mourning ribbon, a printed railroad timetable, or an original carte de visite of one of the hearses to turn up at an out-of-print bookstore, antique shop, or estate sale located along the old route of the funeral train.

George Harrington could not have foreseen it, but when he planned the state funeral for Abraham Lincoln, he was planning the funeral for a future president, too—one destined to be elevated to that office a century after Lincoln's election, and who, like Father Abraham, would die by an assassin's hand. On November 22, 1963, when President John F. Kennedy's body was flown from Dallas, Texas, to Washington,

D.C., Jacqueline Kennedy, still wearing the bright pink suit stained with her husband's blood, stepped off the presidential jet. The chief of protocol asked how he might serve her. She asked that her husband's funeral be modeled on Abraham Lincoln's.

A few nights later, after the funeral at Arlington National Cemetery, as the motorcade headed back to the White House, Jacqueline Kennedy's car broke away from the others. After her vehicle crossed Memorial Bridge, it turned left. Ahead, the thirty-six huge, snowy, marble columns glowed like a classical Greek temple. Mrs. Kennedy's car braked to a stop on the plaza, and she gazed up at the sculpture of Abraham Lincoln enshrined in his memorial. Like Abraham Lincoln, Jefferson Davis became a greater legend in death than he had been in life. After he fell from power, his stock rose in the South—"He suffered for us"—and he became not only the defeated Confederacy's representative man, but also the living catalyst for a new movement, the Lost Cause. He symbolized this movement's collective dream: The South may have lost the war, but it was not wrong, and even in defeat it shone with honor and remained the superior civilization. During Davis's 1886–87 speaking tour, he soared to new heights of glory, surpassing the prestige and fame he once possessed as president of the Confederate States of America. In his old age, it seemed, the South could not have loved him more. Until he died, that is.

The death of Jefferson Davis in 1889 caused a convulsion of emotion and memory. His funeral, like Lincoln's, represented not just the passing of one man but of an era. Four years after Davis died, the funeral train that carried his body from New Orleans to Richmond roused the South and stunned the North. Once more, Americans stood beside railroad tracks, holding signs, bearing torches, and igniting bonfires, waiting for a train to pass by. A tumultuous response welcomed him back to the old capital, where he would reign forever over the dreams of a lost cause. In the 1890s, the White House of the Confederacy was transformed into the Museum of the Confederacy, a shrinelike repository for treasured battle flags, war artifacts, and memories. In 1907, when three hundred and twenty-five thousand people turned out for the dedication of his monument in Richmond, Davis was at the apex of his fame. On that day, his partisans were sure that his name would endure forever and that history would honor him, no less than Lincoln, as a great American.

They were wrong. The twentieth century came to belong to Abraham Lincoln, not Jefferson Davis. His eclipse began as early as 1922, with the completion of the Lincoln Memorial. Before then, two monuments had been erected for Davis in Richmond, one at his gravesite in Hollywood Cemetery and the other on Monument Avenue.

But the Lincoln Memorial overshadowed these Richmond monuments in physical scale and symbolism. It represented the growing power of the Lincoln legend and the Northern interpretation of the War of the Rebellion. It would not have surprised Davis to know that on the day former president William Howard Taft presented the memorial to President Warren G. Harding, with Abraham Lincoln's son Robert looking on, blacks in attendance were forced to sit in segregated seating. Davis had been dubious of how blacks would fare in postwar America. He believed that once the Union freed the slaves, the North would not welcome them as neighbors or equal citizens. Instead, Davis suspected, Northerners viewed blacks as an abstraction, as a convenient cause they would abandon after the war. Racism and hatred, Davis suggested, were not exclusively Southern phenomena. It took a different kind of Southern senator and president—Lyndon B. Johnson—to redeem Lincoln's promise that had been denied during dedication day, on the steps of his own memorial.

Southerners continued to memorialize Jefferson Davis. His capture site languished in obscurity for years and was, in time, overgrown by pines and brush. It was a quiet, forgotten place. This was no landmark of Confederate glory, and few Southerners cared to visit the spot where Davis's presidency and their last hope for independence had died. At some point, Davis loyalists marked the place when they hammered into the ground a wooden stake nailed to a crude, handmade sign that said: SITE OF JEFFERSON DAVIS' CAMP AT THE TIME OF CAPTURE, MAY 10, 1865.

On June 3, 1936, seventy-one years after the end of the Civil War, and the 128th anniversary of Jefferson Davis's birthday, the ladies of the United Daughters of the Confederacy, Ocilla, Georgia Chapter, dedicated a handsome monument at the site. Consisting of a large concrete slab bearing a concrete plaque sculpted in bas relief, with a bronze bust of Davis, the main text of the memorial reads: "Jefferson Davis—President of the Confederate States of America. 1861–1865." This monument was meant to celebrate not capture, defeat, or imprisonment, but the "unconquerable heart" of the man who, in enduring those trials, became a beloved symbol to his people.

Other monuments to Davis mark the landscape near his birthplace in Kentucky, and in his home state of Mississippi. At the U.S. Capitol, a larger-than-life bronze sculpture of Davis stands in National Statuary Hall, its presence a tribute to two things: his service as a U.S. senator and his significant influence on the architecture and modern-day appearance of the Capitol building.

In 2009, America celebrated Abraham Lincoln's two hundredth birthday with great fanfare. President and Mrs. George W. Bush hosted several pre-bicentennial events, including the first black-tie White House dinner ever held in Lincoln's honor. The Library of Congress and the Smithsonian National Museum of American History mounted major exhibitions. The Ford's Theatre Society raised fifty million dollars to renovate the theater and its museum in time for Lincoln's birthday on February 12. The Newseum, located on a stretch of Pennsylvania Avenue overlooking the route of the April 19, 1865, funeral procession, offered an exhibition on the assassination, mourning pageant, and manhunt for Lincoln's killer. Museums in several other cities also put on exhibitions. Filmmakers produced several documentaries, and in 2008 and 2009, authors published nearly one hundred books on the sixteenth president. The U.S. Mint and Post Office produced commemorative coins and stamps.

On June 3, 2008, another bicentennial passed almost without notice. Not many Americans were aware of, let alone chose to celebrate, the two hundredth birthday of Jefferson Davis. There were no White House dinners, major exhibitions, shelves of new books, or coins and stamps. Few people know his story. Most have never read a book about him, and no one reads his memoirs anymore. Many people would not recognize his face, and some would not even remember his name. Jefferson Davis is the lost man of American history.

What explains the rise and fall of Davis in American popular memory? He lost, and history tends to reward winners, not losers. But there must be more to it than that. Perhaps it comes down to the slaves, the song, and the flag. The Confederate past is controversial. In the spring of 2010, on the eve of the 150th anniversary of the Civil War, the governor of Virginia created a furor by proclaiming Confederate History Month, a celebration condemned by some as, at best, insensitive and, at worst, racist. A historical figure who owned slaves, wished he "was in the land of cotton," and waved the Stars and Bars must today be rebuked and erased from popular memory, not studied. Better to forget.

Perhaps, someday, someone will demand that his statue be banished from the U.S. Capitol. In Richmond, the Confederate White House and the Museum of the Confederacy, two of the finest Civil War sites in the country, are in trouble. Once central to that city's identity, they now languish in semi-obscurity, overshadowed physically by an ugly complex of medical office buildings and challenged symbolically by a competing, sleek new Civil War museum at the Tredegar Iron Works, the former cannon manufactory. The Museum of the Confederacy has fallen on hard times and into local disfavor, dismissed by some as an antiquarian dinosaur, by others as an embarrassing reminder of the racial politics of the Lost Cause. Its very name angers some who insist that perpetuating these places of Confederate history is tantamount to a modern-day endorsement of secession, slavery, and racism. According to numerous newspaper stories, the Museum and the White House are barely hanging on, and have considered closing, or dividing the price-less collection among several institutions. Their failure would be a loss to American history. Unless a benefactor comes forward to save them, their long-term future remains uncertain.

There was one place where the legacy of Jefferson Davis was safe, at his beloved postwar sanctuary, Beauvoir. There, on the Mississippi Gulf, he had found the peace that had eluded him during his presidency and during his unsettled postwar wanderings. In an outbuilding, a three-room cottage he set up as his study, he shelved hundreds of books and piled more on tables. A photograph preserves the interior of this time capsule: books everywhere, his desk and chair where he sat and composed his letters and articles and where he wrote *The Rise and Fall of the Confederate Government.*

After Davis's death, Beauvoir lived on as a monument, and it became a retirement home for aged Confederate veterans who came to live there. When the last of them died off, Beauvoir became a Davis museum and library. The institution flourished for decades until one day in late August 2005, when Hurricane Katrina hit the Mississippi Gulf Coast hard. The main house, a lovely, nine-room Gothic cottage set upon pillars, was gutted down to the walls and all seven of the outbuildings were destroyed. Countless artifacts were lost, including Davis's Mexican War saddle, as well as the notorious raglan and shawl he wore on the morning he was captured.

His library did not escape the hurricane either. On that day, the sanctuary where Jefferson Davis labored to preserve for all time the memory of the Confederacy, its honored dead, and the Lost Cause was, by wind and water, all swept away.

A NOTE TO THE READER

The spring of 1865 remains the most remarkable season in American history. It was a time to mourn the Civil War's 620,000 dead. The war was ending. It was a time to lay down arms, to count up plantations and cities laid to waste, and to plant new crops. It was a time of two presidents on their final journeys, of the hunt for Jefferson Davis and the funeral pageant for Abraham Lincoln.

The title of the adult version of this book, *Bloody Crimes*, was inspired by three sources. First, in October 1859, in an attempt to start a slave uprising, **abolitionist** John Brown launched a doomed raid on the U.S. arsenal at Harper's Ferry, Virginia. Brown was captured, tried, and sentenced to hang. While in jail he marked his favorite passages in a copy of the Bible, including this verse from Ezekiel 7:23: "Make a chain: for the land is full of bloody crimes, and the city is full of violence." On the morning he was hanged, he handed to one of his jailers the last note he would ever write, preceding the outbreak of the war by two years. "I, John Brown, am now quite *certain* that the crimes of this *guilty land* will never be purged away but with *blood.*"

Second, on March 4, 1865, Abraham Lincoln delivered a speech to mark the start of his second term as president. Lincoln warned that slavery was a bloody crime that might not be wiped out without the shedding of more blood. "Fondly do we hope," he declared, "fervently do we pray—that this mighty scourge of war may speedily pass away. Yet, if God wills that it continue . . . until every drop of blood drawn with the lash, shall be paid by another drawn with the sword, as was said three thousand years ago, so still it must be said 'the judgments of the Lord, are true and righteous altogether.'"

Third, within days of Lincoln's assassination on April 14, 1865, a Boston photographer published a remarkable image to honor the fallen president. A stern-faced woman, a symbol of the United States, along with an eagle about to take flight in pursuit of its prey, keeps a vigil over a portrait of the murdered president and proclaims John Brown's old warning: "Make a chain, for the land is full of bloody crimes."

Northerners believed that Jefferson Davis and the Confederacy had committed many bloody crimes, including the assassination of Abraham Lincoln, the starvation, torture, and murder of Union prisoners of war, and the battlefield slaughter of soldiers. In the South Lincoln and his armies were seen as guilty of great crimes as well. The people of the Union and the Confederacy could agree about one thing. In the spring of 1865, an era of bloody times had reached its climax.

Entered according to Act of Congress, in the year 1865, by H. W. Horton, in the
Clerk's Office of the District Court for the District of Massachusetts.

"Make a chain, for the land is full of Bloody Crimes."

WHO'S WHO

CONFEDERACY

Judah Benjamin: Confederate secretary of state

John C. Breckinridge: Confederate secretary of war

Constance Cary: a young woman living in Richmond, Virginia, during the Civil War; married to Burton Harrison after the war

Jefferson Davis: president of the Confederate States of America, 1861–1865

Jefferson (Jeff) Davis, Jr.: son of Jefferson and Varina Davis; eight years old in 1865

Margaret (Maggie) Davis: daughter of Jefferson and Varina Davis; ten years old in 1865

Varina Davis: wife of Jefferson Davis

Wade Hampton: Confederate cavalry general, under the command of General Joseph Johnston

Burton Harrison: Jefferson Davis's private secretary; engaged to Constance Cary

Joseph Johnston: Confederate general of the Department of South Carolina, Georgia, and Florida and the Department of North Carolina and Southern Virginia

Jim Jones: Jefferson Davis's coachman

Robert E. Lee: general of the Army of Northern Virginia

Frank Lubbock: former governor of Texas

Stephen R. Mallory: Confederate secretary of the navy

William Parker: Confederate naval captain, in charge of guarding the Confederate treasure train

John Reagan: postmaster general

UNION

Phineas Taylor (P. T.) Barnum: owner of the American Museum in New York City, and later, of the Barnum & Bailey Greatest Show on Earth circus

Dr. Charles Brown: embalmer

John Brown: leader of a raid on a government arsenal, or place where weapons were stored, at Harper's Ferry, Virginia, in 1859. He hoped to use the weapons to arm slaves in a rebellion against their owners. He was captured, tried, and executed.

William Clarke: a boarder at the Petersen house in Washington, D.C.

Charles Crane: assistant surgeon general

Elizabeth Dixon: friend of Mary Lincoln

George Francis: a boarder at the Petersen house in Washington, D.C.; husband of Huldah Francis

Huldah Francis: a boarder at the Petersen house in Washington, D.C.; wife of George Francis

Benjamin Brown French: commissioner of public buildings and grounds in Washington, D.C.

Ulysses S. Grant: general of the Armies of the United States

George Harrington: United States assistant secretary of the treasury; in charge of organizing Lincoln's funeral in Washington, D.C.

Clara Harris: fiancée of Henry Rathbone

Elizabeth Keckly: dressmaker, friend of Mary Lincoln

Charles A. Leale: army surgeon

Abraham Lincoln: president of the United States, 1861–1865

Edward (Eddie) Lincoln: son of Abraham and Mary Lincoln; died in 1850 at the age of three

Mary Lincoln: wife of Abraham Lincoln

Robert Lincoln: son of Abraham and Mary Lincoln; twenty-one years old in 1865

Thomas (Tad) Lincoln: son of Abraham and Mary Lincoln; twelve years old in 1865

William (Willie) Lincoln: son of Abraham and Mary Lincoln; died in 1862 at the age of eleven

David Dixon Porter: rear admiral, U.S. Navy

Benjamin D. Pritchard: United States lieutenant colonel in command of the Fourth Michigan Cavalry unit that captured Jefferson Davis

Alfred Purington: United States lieutenant serving in the Fourth Michigan Cavalry unit that captured Jefferson Davis

Henry Rathbone: United States army major, married to Clara Harris after the war

Henry Safford: a boarder at the Petersen house in Washington, D.C.

Frank Sands: undertaker

William Seward: United States secretary of state

William T. Sherman: One of Lincoln's top three generals, along with Grant and Sheridan, and known for "Sherman's March" through the deep South to the sea

Edwin M. Stanton: United States secretary of war

Edward Townsend: United States brigadier general; in command of Abraham Lincoln's funeral train

Gideon Welles: United States secretary of the navy

Mary Jane Welles: wife of Gideon Welles

Janvier Woodward: doctor; participated in the autopsy on Lincoln's body

GLOSSARY

abolitionist: someone who opposes slavery and works to end it

bier: a table or platform on which a coffin is laid

cabinet: a group of the most important officials in a government and advisers to the president

carbine: lightweight rifle with a short barrel

cavalry: soldiers mounted on horseback

choice: fine, special

Confederate: belonging to or connected with the Confederate States of America, the independent country that the South of the United

States attempted to create during the Civil War

conscripts: soldiers who have been drafted or forced to fight

Constitution: the ultimate law of the United States. All laws made by Congress must abide by what is written in the Constitution.

coveted: strongly wanted or desired

crepe: a lightweight, fine fabric. When black, it was often used to symbolize death or mourning.

Declaration of Independence: the statement of the United States' freedom from England and its existence as an independent country

dirge: sad music played at a funeral

dormant: not active, but able to become active later

embalmer: someone who preserves a body for viewing before burial

extricate: take out, remove

fatigue: the state of being tired or exhausted

fortitude: strength, endurance

guerrilla warfare: war fought by sabotage and secret attacks rather than conflict on the battlefield between armies

haversack: backpack

illumination: celebration during which buildings are lit up with lamps, lanterns, or candles

malaria: a disease caused by the bite of a mosquito. An infected person often suffers from chills and fevers.

motto: brief phrase or statement, often written on a banner or flag

neuralgia: severe pain that occurs from time to time in a particular part of the body

reconstruction: the process of rebuilding something that has been destroyed or damaged

subsistence: food or supplies, just enough to keep someone or something alive

treasury: place where a government's money is stored

uniform: regular, unchanging

Union: belonging to or connected with the northern part of the United States during the Civil War, which wanted to keep the country together and not divide it into two separate countries

United States Congress: the part of the government that makes laws for the United States. The Congress has two parts, the Senate and the House of Representatives.

United States Senate: one of the two bodies that make up the U.S. Congress

utterance: speech

venerable: respected, honored

FOR FURTHER READING

There are thousands of books about Abraham Lincoln, and even more about the Civil War. Here are a few titles for anyone who would like to pursue the stories of Abraham Lincoln and Jefferson Davis in more detail. Readers of *Bloody Times: The Funeral of Abraham Lincoln and the Manhunt for Jefferson Davis* who want to learn more about the Lincoln funeral and Davis manhunt can move up to the adult book upon which is it based, *Bloody Crimes: The Chase for Jefferson Davis and the Death Pageant for Lincoln's Corpse*. *Bloody Crimes* also contains an extensive bibliography for further reading. For the story of the Lincoln assassination and the hunt for John Wilkes Booth, see my young adult book *Chasing Lincoln's Killer*, or its adult version, *Manhunt: The 12-Day Chase for Lincoln's Killer*.

There are no completely satisfactory biographies of Abraham Lincoln or Jefferson Davis for young adults. Their stories are almost too detailed and complex to reduce them to short books that can only highlight the most important themes. The moment a young reader is ready to tackle an adult biography on Lincoln, I recommend Benjamin Thomas's classic work, *Abraham Lincoln*. For the best illustrated books on the Lincoln assassination, see *Twenty Days: A Narrative in Text and Pictures of the Assassination of Abraham Lincoln* by Dorothy Meserve Kunhardt and Philip B. Kunhardt Jr., and my full-color book *Lincoln's Assassins: Their Trial and Execution*. The best general photographic history is Lloyd Ostendorf's *Lincoln's Photographs: A Complete Album*.

To find all of Abraham Lincoln's letters, speeches, and other writings, the best source is the multivolume set edited by Roy P. Basler, *The Collected Works of Abraham Lincoln*. For the multivolume collected works of Lincoln's opponent, see Lynda Lasswell Crist's *The Papers of Jefferson Davis*. The best adult biography of Jefferson Davis is William J. Cooper's *Jefferson Davis, American*. The ultimate book on Lincoln is Michael Burlingame's magnificent two-volume biography, *Abraham Lincoln: A Life*. Too detailed and expensive for the home bookshelves of young readers, Burlingame's work is an invaluable, encyclopedic library resource for anyone researching the Lincoln story.

PLACES TO GO

Today you can visit many of the places that you have read about in *Bloody Times*. In Washington, D.C., Ford's Theatre still stands on Tenth Street, and looks exactly like it did on April 14, 1865, the night Abraham Lincoln was shot. Go inside the theater, and while you listen to a talk by a National Park Service ranger, look up at the box where John Wilkes Booth shot the president and then leaped to the stage below. Be sure to visit the splendid museum in the basement and view, among the treasured relics there, Booth's compass, revolvers, knives, and carbine, and even the very derringer pistol he used to assassinate Abraham Lincoln. Do not leave Tenth Street without visiting the Petersen House, where the president died on the morning of April 15.

In Washington you can walk up Pennsylvania Avenue from the White House to the U.S. Capitol, the same route followed by Abraham Lincoln's funeral procession on April 19, 1865. Along the way, you will pass Mathew Brady's old photography studio, which Lincoln visited many times to pose for pictures. At the U.S. Capitol, if you stand at the center of the rotunda, directly below the Great Dome, you will be in the exact spot where Abraham Lincoln's coffin once rested, and where tens of thousands of mourners passed by to view his body. Nearby, in Statuary Hall, see if you can find the large, bronze sculpture of Jefferson Davis, former United States senator from Mississippi. There is a fine Lincoln exhibition at the Smithsonian National Museum of American History, and, near Ford's Theatre at the National Portrait Gallery, in a building where Lincoln held his second inaugural ball, you will find an excellent display on the Civil War.

In Springfield, Illinois, you can visit the Old State Capitol where Lincoln served as a legislator, the Abraham Lincoln Presidential Library and Museum, his home, one of his law offices, and his tomb, which is far grander than anything Lincoln himself would have ever wanted. Do not leave Springfield without visiting New Salem, the nearby pioneer village where Lincoln worked as a postmaster as a young man.

In Richmond, Virginia, be sure to visit the Museum of the Confederacy and, next door, the White House of the Confederacy, two of the finest Civil War sites in America. The museum displays hundreds of flags, uniforms, firearms, swords, and other relics. The White House looks almost exactly like it did when President Davis, his wife, Varina, and their young children lived there. If you go to Richmond's famous Hollywood Cemetery, you will discover not only the graves of Jefferson Davis and his family, but those of Presidents James Monroe and John Tyler. And on Monument Avenue stand sculptures of President Davis, Robert E. Lee, and other Confederate leaders.

Near Biloxi, Mississippi, Jefferson's Davis's last home, Beauvoir, has been restored after having been damaged by Hurricane Katrina in 2005.

In Georgia, at the lonely site near Irwinville where Jefferson Davis was captured on May 10, 1865, you will find a monument and small museum.

These are just a few of the places where the Civil War, and the lives of Abraham Lincoln and Jefferson Davis, unfolded.

ACKNOWLEDGMENTS

My wife, Andrea E. Mays, although busy writing her own book on the hunt for the rare, surviving copies of Shakespeare's first folio, which collected his plays in 1623, seven years after his death, thus saving many of them from being lost forever, read the manuscript for *Bloody Times* several times and made numerous editorial suggestions and improvements. Our boys, Harrison and Cameron, ages twelve and thirteen, are my top advisors on writing for young people. They are our companions on visits to historic sites, my assistants at book signings, and coaches on storytelling. "Readers want blood," said Cameron. "And knives," added Harrison.

My agent, Richard Abate, encouraged me to reach out to a wider audience and write books not only for adults, but also for young people. One of the great pleasures of writing my first young adult book, *Chasing Lincoln's Killer*, was to meet so many young adults who share a love of American history. I look forward to meeting more of you through the publication of *Bloody Times*.

I thank all my friends at HarperCollins for their hard work. I owe special thanks to my editors Phoebe Yeh and Alyson Day for their enthusiasm, support, and excellent work in translating my adult book *Bloody Crimes: The Chase for Jefferson Davis and the Death Pageant for Lincoln's Corpse* into the book you now hold in your hands. In the immortal words of Abraham Lincoln, they exerted "the last full measure of devotion" in bringing this book to publication. And thanks to Tom Forget for designing the beautiful cover.

I wish that I could thank by name the many librarians, archivists, scholars, and curators who have assisted my research. I must, however, thank my friends at the Library of Congress, the Museum of the Confederacy, the Jefferson Davis home at Beauvoir, and the Papers of Jefferson Davis project for special assistance.

Finally, my father, Lennart Swanson, traveled with me for much of my journey back in time to Civil War America. In a way, he began this book by taking me on an unforgettable trip to Gettysburg when I was ten years old. We have been traveling on that path together ever since.

James L. Swanson
Washington, D.C.
November 2010